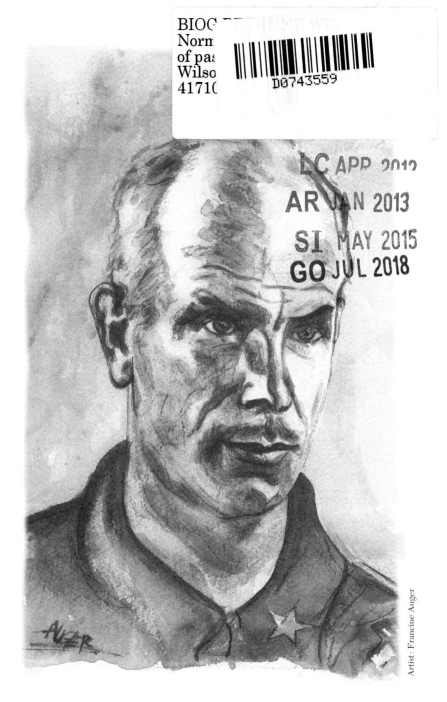

Artist : Francine Auger

Norman Bethune, 1890-1939.

John Wilson

John Wilson is the author of six books for young adults and one work of adult historical fiction, *North with Franklin: The Lost Journals of James Fitzjames* (Fitzhenry & Whiteside). His books for children include *Across Frozen Seas* (Beach Holme), which was shortlisted for both the Sheila Egoff and Geoffrey Bilson prizes; *Lost in Spain* (Fitzhenry & Whiteside), a tale set in the Spanish Civil War; and the *Weet* trilogy (Napoleon). His short story, "Shadows of the Past," was included in the 1998 anthology *Winds Through Time* (Beach Holme).

An ex-Research Geologist, John has travelled extensively and published over three hundred magazine and newspaper feature articles on subjects as diverse as the ruined cities of Thailand and the pitfalls of educating children. He has had more than thirty poems published in literary magazines, and he regularly reviews both adult and children's books for *Quill & Quire*. John enjoys giving readings, presentations, and workshops in schools and at book festivals and writing conferences. He lives with his family in Lantzville on Vancouver Island. Comments on his books may be sent to John at wilsonj@nanaimo.ark.com.

Norman Bethune

Canadian Cataloguing in Publication Data

Wilson, John, 1951-

    Norman Bethune : a life of passionate conviction

    (The Quest Library ; 1)
    Includes bibliographical references and index.

    ISBN 0-9683601-1-4

    1. Bethune, Norman, 1890-1939. 2. Surgeons – Canada – Biography. 3. Surgeons – China – Biography. 4. Surgeons – Spain – Biography. I. Title. II. Series.

R464.B4W54 1999   617'.092   C99-941234-5

Legal Deposit: Fourth quarter 1999
National Library of Canada
Bibliothèque nationale du Québec

XYZ Publishing acknowledges the support of The Quest Library project by the Canadian Studies Program and the Book Publishing Industry Development Program (BPIDP) of the Department of Canadian Heritage. The opinions expressed do not necessarily reflect the views of the Government of Canada.

The publishers further acknowledge the financial support our publishing program receives from The Canada Council for the Arts, the ministère de la Culture et des Communications du Québec, and the Société de développement des entreprises culturelles.

Chronology and Index: Lynne Bowen
Layout: Édiscript enr.
Cover design: Zirval Design
Cover illustration: Francine Auger

Printed and bound in Canada

XYZ Publishing
1781 Saint Hubert Street
Montreal, Quebec   H2L 3Z1
Tel: (514) 525-2170
Fax: (514) 525-7537
E-mail: xyzed@mlink.net

Distributed by: General Distribution Services
325 Humber College Boulevard
Toronto, Ontario   M9W 7C3
Tel: (416) 213-1919
Fax: (416) 213-1917
E-mail: cservice@genpub.com

BETHUNE

Norman

A LIFE OF PASSIONATE CONVICTION

XYZ Publishing

In memory of
Helen Margaret (Eelin) Beardall,
1931-1999, who also
devoted her life to others.

Contents

Editor's Note

In this book we have chosen to use the spellings that Norman Bethune used for names of historical figures and geographical place names. Where the spellings of names of historical figures or major place names have changed since Bethune's time, we have made note of the current spelling when the name is first mentioned in the story and in the chronology.

With a new Renault truck to carry supplies or refugees,
Bethune is ready to travel the Malaga road. Spain, 1937.

Prologue

The Malaga Road

After the planes had passed I picked up in my arms three dead children from the pavement…where they had been standing in a great queue waiting for a cupful of preserved milk and a handful of dry bread…. One's body felt as heavy as the dead themselves, but empty and hollow, and in one's brain burned a bright flame of hate.

D r. Norman Bethune was faced with an impossible decision – who to save and who to let die? He was surrounded by frantic people – mothers, children, grandfathers – all exhausted, hungry, and thirsty, united only in the common terror that had driven them from their homes to flee for four days and nights along the road to safety. Many could barely walk and there was still a long way to go. Bethune might be their salvation, or at least the salvation of their children.

"Take this one."

"See this child."

"This one is wounded."

They shouted their pleas at him. How could he possibly choose? Was a child more deserving of life than an old woman? He saw a mother carrying a newborn infant. She had stopped walking only long enough to give birth to the baby by the side of the road. He saw a woman of sixty unable to stagger another step. She had swollen legs, and open sores bled into her linen sandals. He saw people who had given up and who lay quietly by the roadside awaiting death.

It was late in the evening of Wednesday, February 10, 1937. The Spanish Civil War was already almost seven months old, and the elected Republican government was struggling against a fascist insurrection led by General Franco. Bethune was standing on the running board of a two-and-a-half-ton Renault truck full of blood and medical supplies. With his assistant Hazen Sise and the English writer Tom Worsley, he had been driving since 6:00 p.m. along the narrow coast road from Almeria to Malaga in southern Spain. Now they could go no farther. The road was jammed with a human caterpillar of distress. The thousands of people crammed together reminded Bethune of bees swarming in a hive; the hum of their voices filled the air.

Bethune had intended to provide blood transfusion services to the Republican soldiers wounded in the fighting to save Malaga – but he was too late. After weeks of bombing and shelling, Malaga had fallen to the fascists several days before. When Bethune had heard the news in Almeria that afternoon, he had decided to press on as far as possible along the 169-kilometre road to Malaga to help what wounded he could find.

The fighting was over, but the killing was still going on. Even as Bethune was deciding what to do, government sympathizers who had remained in Malaga were being herded onto the famous tourist beaches of the Costa del Sol and shot. At the southern end of the pitiful refugee column, fascist soldiers were dragging the men off the road and shooting them in the fields, in full view of their horrified families. The women and children were being allowed to continue their sad trek because the fascists wanted them to become a burden on the already overstretched resources of the Spanish Republic.

As Bethune looked about, his decision was made for him. A man held out a skinny, fever-ridden child and begged, "My child is very ill.... He will die before I carry him to Almeria.... Take him – leave him wherever there is a hospital.... Tell them this one is Juan Blas and that I will come soon to find him."

Bethune placed the child on the seat. Around him others were shouting now. "Take our women and children...the fascists will be upon us soon."

"Have pity *camarada*, save us, for the love of God."

"Let us go with your vehicle, we can walk no further."

"Camarada, *los niños* – the children."

Bethune was overwhelmed with bitterness and anger at an uncaring world. Afterwards, he wrote: "Where are they tonight, the appointed ministers to the Christian God, bearers on earth of His love and salvation – where are they that they hear nothing of those who cry out to their Lord?... If only I had a thousand pairs of hands, and in each hand a thousand deadly guns, and for each gun a thousand bullets, and each bullet marked for an assigned child-killer – then I would know how to speak!... I would roar at the ears of the slumbering world.... 'Your hands are polluted with innocent blood, all you who sleep peacefully tonight! Your cities are Sodom and Gomorrah if you care nothing for the shame on Malaga road tonight!'"

Bethune, Sise, and Worsley unloaded the equipment and blood supplies. The crowd surged forward as the back doors were thrown open.

"*Solamente niños. Niños!* Children only!"

Bethune fought against the ranks of hysterical refugees. The decisions were immediate now – who would go and who would stay? Who to take first? He spotted a woman holding a child and made his way towards her through the throng. "We'll take your child!" he said.

The woman just looked at him and held her child tighter. Bethune thought perhaps she didn't understand. He put out his arms to take the child. The woman made no move, she simply looked at him without expression. The child was too young to be separated from its mother. Suddenly Bethune was uncertain. It was easy to say, "Children only," but if they took this child from its mother, both would probably die. Bethune led them to the truck.

Bethune worked constantly, every choice a nightmare. He tried to soothe the women. He carried children in his arms. Grimly, he turned the adults away. Groups of mothers stood in knots, whispering. Some men, realizing that they could not go, drifted off in despair into the surrounding fields. Bethune was tortured by the decisions he had to make. He had no way of knowing this, but his humanitarian selection for life was a grim parody in reverse of the nightmarish selections for death that the fascists themselves would soon be making on the railway platforms of Auschwitz and Treblinka.

The truck was almost full. Now the decisions became even more painful. An old man with tears in his eyes touched Bethune's arm. Bethune shook his head. He couldn't take the man, but the pleading face would haunt his dreams.

The old woman with the bleeding legs was there. She was somebody's mother. Bethune felt sympathy. The woman looked away calmly, asking for nothing.

Bethune picked a little girl from a screaming woman. A small body to fill the last space. He made his way to the truck through the now-silent crowd. In his journal, he described what happened next.

"Suddenly a woman pushed in front of me, seized the door-jambs and clambered into the truck. I caught her ankle in mid-air and swore, but she shook free and turned about in the confined space to face me. 'Get out!' I ordered, holding the child towards her. 'It's you or the child! Do you understand? Will you take the place of the child?'

"The woman was young. Her long black hair fell about her pale face. She looked at me with hunted eyes, then flung open her cloak and raised her cotton shift high. Her belly was distended with child.

"For a moment we looked at each other, I with the child in my arms, she with the child in her womb. She pressed herself down on the tiny space of flooring at her feet, her great stomach between her knees, smiled at me and held out her arms. With her eyes and her arms and her smile she seemed to be saying: 'See, I will take the child, and it will be as if I am not here, as if I am taking nobody's place.' She placed the girl on her knees, pillowing the little head on her shoulders."

Bethune closed the doors. There were forty children and two women jammed into the truck. He ordered Hazen Sise to drive his precious cargo to Almeria, drop them at the hospital, and return. Then he and Worsley joined the long trek, tending to the injured where they could, and helping the weakest manage a few more kilometres. Bethune helped the old woman with the bleeding legs to walk for two hours until she could go no farther. Then he made a bed for her in an open field. As he left her, he wondered if she would be picked up by someone else or if the fascists would reach her first.

By midnight he had been walking for four hours and was amazed at how those around him had managed this for four days. The last bandage had been put on a wound; the last pill administered; the last chocolate bar given away; the last cigarette smoked. Bethune threw away his empty kit. He had only his bare hands as he waited impatiently for Sise to return. Then he would begin again. *It is like trying to drain an ocean with a thimble*, he thought.

Sise returned, and for four days and nights they ferried into Almeria those too weak to walk any farther. They didn't sleep. They lost all track of time. On the second day they began taking whole families. They ran out of food. Almost magically, a street hawker appeared with a cart of oranges. Bethune bought them all and, keeping only one for himself, distributed the rest. By day it was so hot that the sun blistered their skin. At night it was so cold that they longed for the sun.

Later, Bethune recalled a great silence settling over the refugees. "The starving lay in the fields, gripped by torpor, stirring themselves only to nibble at fugitive weeds. The thirsty sat on the rocks, trembling, or staggered about aimlessly, the wild glassy stare of delusion in their eyes. The dead lay indiscriminately among the sick, looking unblinkingly into the sun. Then the planes swept overhead – glinting, silvery Italian fighters and squadrons of German Heinkels. They dived towards the road, as casually as at target-practice, their machine guns weaving intricate geometric patterns about the fleeing refugees."

At last they could do no more. Almeria had become a huge camp. Thousands of people were sleeping in the streets and the town square. Bethune collapsed on a cot in an improvised hospital for children. He managed to sleep for only one hour before he was wrenched back to the present by a wailing air-raid siren. The following day he wrote about what happened next.

"I scrambled to my feet, and fell on my knees again as the first bomb went off.... I scrambled up again, the floor still vibrating under my feet. More explosions sounded, some nearby, some distant.

"I ran through the dark corridors, jostling against people hurrying in every direction. In the dormitories children were crying with fright. I found my way into the street, and made for the centre of the city on the run.

"The planes kept sweeping in, one after another, the roar of the engines filling the street until it seemed my eardrums would burst. Then came the bombs, falling up ahead.

"I caught a glimpse of one bomber banking gracefully in the moonlight, disdaining the protection of height or darkness. The devils could afford to take their time! The occasional burst of anti-aircraft fire merely prettied up the sky like roman candles.

"In a few minutes I reached the densely populated section of the city. Here the streets were no longer dark. Great sheets of flame shot up from the skeletons of buildings, hit by incendiaries. In the glare of the burning buildings, as far as the eye could see, vast crowds of people surged about wildly, running from the bombs, going down under toppling walls, falling, crawling, disappearing into bombpits, clutching and screaming as they vanished.

"There were no sounds of bombing from the direction of the port. The bombers weren't interested in the port! They were after human prey. They were after the hundred thousand people who had eluded them at Malaga, who had refused to live under the fascists, who were now penned together here in a perfect target. For a week they had let Almeria alone. For a week they had prepared. Now that the trek from Malaga was over, now that the refugees were caught in a few city blocks where mass murder required only a minimum number of bombs – now Franco was slaking his thirst for revenge. He cared little for the port. A port couldn't think, defy fascism or bleed. Only people had brains, hearts, courage. Kill them, maim them, show them the merciless claw of fascism.…

"I fought my way through the dense crowds, shouting, '*Medico! Medico!*' My voice lost in the shrieking of the sirens, the explosions, the fearful braying of donkeys impaling themselves on twisted railings.

"Then suddenly the bombing stopped and the roar of the planes faded away in the sky. The flaming buildings lit up the faces of men and women looking numbed, shocked, horror stricken.…

"The raid was over. My ears ached in the silence. Silence? No. With the bombing over I could hear the voices…the raid was over, but the dead and dying remained.

"I bound the wounds of the injured with strips of cotton torn from their shirts. In a gutted house I found a little girl whimpering beneath a pile of heavy beams. She was perhaps three years old. I pulled the beams away and carried her in my arms till I came across an emergency ambulance. I laid her on a stretcher, thinking it would be kinder if she died, for if the crippled body survived, the light of sanity had gone out of her childish eyes."

There is no way of knowing what happened to the little girl, or the woman with the bleeding legs, or Juan Blas. Perhaps they survived, perhaps not. If they did, it was in large part due to Bethune's courage and flexibility in a time of crisis.

Bethune survived Spain, but his experiences on the Malaga road and the memory of the bombing of the refugees in Almeria fueled the "bright flame of hate" in his mind. After the Malaga road, Bethune threw himself into the struggle against fascism with a hectic passion that led directly to his death less than three years later. However, his lifelong struggle against injustice had always been very personal, and it had its roots deep in the Ontario wilderness and late in the previous century.

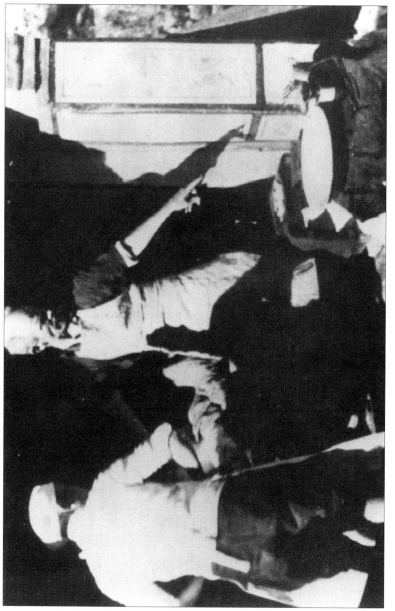

Bethune points with a gloveless hand during an operation in a Buddhist Temple, Hopei, China, 1939.

1

Death and Birth

You must remember my father was an evangelist and I come of a race of men violent, unstable, of passionate conviction and wrong headedness, intolerant yet with it all a vision of truth and a drive to carry them on to it even though it leads, as it has done in my family, to their own destruction.

Today, if you contract septicemia – blood poisoning – from an infected cut on your finger, a short course of antibiotics will cure you. Even on its own, the body of a healthy individual can often muster enough resources to fight off the infection. If, however, there are no antibiotics and your body is weakened from poor diet, sleep deprivation, and overwork, you are doomed.

First your finger will become inflamed, swollen, and painful. Slowly the inflammation will spread up your arm until the arm is useless and you are in agony. You will suffer severe headaches, periods of delirium, high fever, chills, and weakness. Nothing will stay in your stomach and you will retch continuously.

In your blood the bacteria will release toxins, which will trigger your body's immune response and clot the blood – your blood will coagulate in your veins. After several days of this misery, you will go into septic shock. It will be the end.

This was how Norman Bethune died, in a peasant's hut in the remote mountains of northern China. It was 5:20 on the morning of November 12, 1939.

Fifteen days before, Bethune had operated on a soldier with a broken leg. He was tired, but that wasn't unusual, for he was driving himself hard. As he worked, the chisel he was using slipped and sliced open the middle finger of his left hand. This too was not unusual. There were no surgical gloves and, in any case, Bethune preferred working without them. He said it gave him more sensitivity. Minor accidents with the sharp surgical instruments were quite common. A nurse bandaged the finger and Bethune continued.

But something different happened this time. Several days later, Bethune operated, again barehanded, on a soldier with a long-untreated head wound. The wound was infected with streptococcus. By November 5, Bethune's finger was swollen and he was running a fever. Despite that, when he heard guns in the distance, he mounted his horse and led his surgical team toward the fighting. But the blood poisoning was working on him. The local commander ordered Bethune back to the village of Huang-shih K'ou.

Now he was seriously ill. The only thing he would eat was persimmon fruit supplied by the son of the family who had taken him in. There was nothing his friends or colleagues could do except watch helplessly as the infection took its course.

Bethune knew what that course was. He addressed his last will to General Nieh, the Commander-in-Chief of the communist forces in the area: "I am fatally ill. I am going to die.... My two cots are for you and Mrs. Nieh. My two pairs of English shoes also go to you.... Dr. Yo is to have eight of my surgical instruments, Dr. Lin eight and Dr. Fong eight. Dr. Chiang...may choose two as souvenirs.... Give my everlasting love to T.B. and all my Canadian and American friends. Tell them I have been very happy.

"My only regret is that I shall now be unable to do more. The last two years have been the most significant, the most meaningful years of my life. Sometimes it has been lonely, but I have found my highest fulfillment here among my beloved comrades.

"I have no strength now to write more..."

In the mountains around Bethune, as he struggled to write on the last night of his life, the soldiers he had spent the last two years tending were shouting his name as they desperately fought the Japanese army that was invading their country.

The Malaga road led Norman Bethune to an unpleasant, lonely death in a remote place no one in

Canada had ever heard of. But the road that brought him to this final destination began long before Bethune went to Spain.

∞

On March 1, 1546, a man stood at a window in St. Andrews Castle on the east coast of Scotland. He was an important man, a cardinal in the Roman Catholic church, Archbishop of St. Andrews, and Chancellor of Scotland. With Mary Queen of Scots still an infant, this man was the virtual ruler of the land. His name was David Beaton.

The scene before the window was of a small open square, which bordered the castle moat. A crowd stood silently around the edges. In the centre stood a raised wooden platform from which rose a single wooden stake. Tied to the stake was a man named George Wishart. He had been sentenced to die on this afternoon because he had dared to speak out against Cardinal Beaton's Catholic faith and in favour of reforming the injustices of the church.

As Beaton watched, a flaming torch was thrust into the kindling piled around Wishart's feet. Crackling flames hungrily ate the dry wood and rose up around the struggling figure. Mercifully, smoke billowed up to hide Wishart's final agonizing moments. Satisfied that his orders had been carried out, Beaton turned away.

David Beaton had inherited much of his power from his uncle, James. Both men were violently opposed to the new Reformation movement that was taking root in the Scottish church. In fact, in 1528, James had been responsible for burning the first Scottish Protestant martyr, Patrick Hamilton. Now, on the same spot where Hamilton died, George Wishart was undergoing his ordeal. But David Beaton had miscalculated. Wishart was a close friend of John Knox, and his death would inspire Knox to lead the Scots away from the Catholic church and towards his own vision of Protestantism. In fact, less than three months after Wishart's death, on May 29, a band of Protestants broke into the castle, murdered Beaton, and threw his body from the very window at which he had stood to watch Wishart burn.

∞

Two days and 344 years after George Wishart met his unpleasant end, another Bethune (as Beaton was now spelled), was born across the ocean in Canada. The clapboard manse in Gravenhurst, a sawmill town one hundred miles (161 km) north of Toronto, still stands. When Henry Norman Bethune drew his first breath in that house, he was setting off on the personal journey that would ultimately lead him to the peasant hut in war-torn China. But the true beginning of his story stretches back to the cruel Beatons and even before.

The Bethunes can trace their name to minor Norman nobility at the time of William the Conqueror. In addition to the incendiary Beatons, the ancestors include a twelfth-century poet, a minister of finance to the King of France, and a handmaid to Mary Queen of Scots.

The branch of the family tree from which Norman descended was less bloodthirsty than some of the others. For four generations the Bethunes practised as surgeons on the Isle of Skye, off the west coast of Scotland. Then, around 1772, John Bethune moved to the American colonies. There is little indication why John made the move. A family story maintains that John's father was wounded fighting with the Scottish Jacobite rebels against the English army at the battle of Culloden Moor in 1746, but there is nothing to suggest that John ever got into any trouble for radical views. The situation changed in America, where John was imprisoned during the Revolutionary War for supporting the side loyal to the British crown.

After he was released, John Bethune fled to Canada, where he lived out a respectable life and became noted for organizing the first Presbyterian congregation in Montreal.

The stark religion of Presbyterianism had few frills in those days. Reverend John Bethune's church was very sparsely furnished. Probably there was no piano or organ because musical instruments distracted from worship. There would not have been any hymns, only the Psalms of David. No carpets, no upholstery, not even any pews, just rough-hewn cedar planks resting on wooden blocks. You didn't go to this church to be comfortable. You went to worship and bare your soul before a stern, unyielding God.

Four generations later, the same focus on the importance of the spiritual over mere physical comfort can be seen in one of Norman Bethune's descriptions of conditions in China. "Why shouldn't I be happy – see what my riches consist of. First I have important work which fully occupies every minute of my time from 5:30 in the morning to 9 at night. I am needed. More than that – to satisfy my bourgeois vanity – the need for me is expressed. I have a cook, a personal servant, my own house, a fine Japanese horse and saddle. I have no money nor the need of it – everything is given me." The cook couldn't boil an egg, the servant had nothing to do, the house was made of mud bricks, and the horse was one of the spoils of war. Great-great-grandfather John would have understood.

One of John's sons, Angus, forsook both the religious and medical callings of his ancestors and opted instead for adventure and commerce. He travelled the world, trapped for furs in the Canadian wilderness, and achieved a prominent position in both the North West and later the Hudson's Bay Companies. But, like his great-grandson Norman, he was not always the easiest of people to get on with. In the journals of his boss, George Simpson, he is characterized as "...a very poor creature, vain, self-sufficient and trifling, who makes his own comfort his principal study, possessing little nerve and no decision in anything...neither liked nor respected by his associates, servants or Indians."

Even in death, the unlikable Angus was controversial. He left almost all of his considerable wealth to only one of his four sons – Norman.

The first Dr. Norman Bethune exhibited many of the characteristics that would be evident in his namesake and grandson. He travelled, was a good surgeon, competent artist and writer, and had difficulty holding on to money. He also ruffled the feathers of those in authority at Trinity College Medical School and Victoria College in Toronto, where he taught and practised. Through bad planning and periods of excessive drinking, he squandered much of his inheritance and died penniless in a home for "incurables" in Toronto in 1892. His last few years were spent living in the household of his second son Malcolm and his wife Elizabeth, and their young son, Henry Norman.

Although Henry Norman was less than three years old when his grandfather died, he claimed to remember him and even copied the old man's limping walk. At the age of eight, he announced that he wanted to be known as Norman, not Henry, and he hung his grandfather's brass plate outside his bedroom door.

As a young man, Norman's father had gone off in search of adventure. At the age of twenty-three Malcolm sailed to Australia, where he tried his hand at sheep farming. The farm failed and the penniless lad was forced to beg his father for money for the passage home. In Hawaii he apparently invested in orange groves, another failed enterprise, but he also met a missionary, Elizabeth Goodwin. Her fire converted the young man to the Presbyterian religion of his forefathers. The pair married, and Malcolm began a long career ministering the gospel to small communities across the northern wilds of Ontario. The zealous evangelist refused positions of greater comfort in favour of appointments to small communities such as Blind River, Owen Sound, and Blackheath. One such appointment was to Gravenhurst, where Malcolm's poverty-stricken father came to live with them and where the couple's first son was born.

Norman Bethune inherited many of the characteristics of his ancestors. He had his parents' sense that those less fortunate could be helped, and like them he was capable of fiery commitment to a cause. He had his grandfather's artistic and literary talents and reckless disregard for money, and he inherited some of Angus Bethune's cantankerous nature and love of adventure. With them all, he shared an unshakable belief that he was right and that his course was the correct one. In Norman, the Bethune family characteristics combined to create an extraordinary man possessed of the power to change the world around him.

The Bethune family, 1904. l-r: Malcolm Goodwin, Elizabeth Ann Goodwin, Henry Norman, Janet Louise. Norman's father is not there to hate.

2

Early Wars

Father and I had our usual hate together.

N orman Bethune liked having his photograph taken. He was vain, and when he lived in the city, he took trouble with his appearance. His clothing was often eccentric, but it was usually immaculate. He wanted to look his best. Even when he went to war, he made sure many pictures were taken of him posing beside his medical units or operating on wounded soldiers.

The earliest surviving photograph of Norman Bethune is a family shot taken around 1894. It shows a light, horse-drawn buggy on a muddy road in one of the Reverend Malcolm's parishes. Bethune's mother sits in the buggy with his older sister, Janet Louise, and his baby brother, Malcolm Goodwin. Beside the horse stands his father, wearing a straw boater and, with his hand placed rakishly on his hip, not looking much like a country parson. Seated bareback upon the horse is Norman. All are dressed in their Sunday best and look directly at the camera. It is a serious, formal occasion and everyone is aware of that. Everyone except Norman. He sits with his head cocked questioningly at the camera and looks as if he is about to flip the reins, dig his heels in to the horse's side, and gallop off into the distance.

On this occasion he did not gallop out of the camera's viewfinder, but his desire to do something different, to push the limits and find out how far he could go, was already strong.

Just three years after the family photograph was taken, the Bethune family moved for a short time to Toronto. The big city was a novelty to the six-year-old Norman, who had only seen small rural towns up until then. One morning he decided to go exploring. At dusk, completely unconcerned that his parents were frantic with worry, he returned and announced that he had walked entirely across the ten-mile-wide city. On another occasion he eluded his mother on a shopping trip just to see what it was like to be lost. After he surrendered to a policeman, he declared that being lost was fun.

No one growing up can ever completely escape the experiences of early childhood. How your parents disciplined and encouraged you, what your interests were, and where you lived all leave an indelible impression. The influences on the young Norman were strong and varied.

Both Norman's parents were fervent believers in goodness and justice. From them, the boy received a sense of right and fairness that never left him. However, their attempts to instill evangelical Christianity in their boy failed.

Elizabeth Bethune was passionately against the teaching of evolution. When Norman brought home a copy of Darwin's *Origin of Species* as a school text, his mother took to placing religious tracts between its pages. In response, Norman sneaked into his mother's room while she slept and slid a copy of Darwin's book beneath her pillow. Elizabeth was not amused, and the book ended up in the woodburning kitchen stove.

The strong-willed Elizabeth was determined to raise an obedient, God-fearing son, and her approach led to numerous conflicts. Oddly, it was with his father that Norman had the most violent disagreements. Perhaps the outspoken son regarded his father's tendency to apologize profusely after one of their fights as a weakness. In any case, their temperaments often clashed. On one occasion Malcolm pushed Norman's face into the ground and forced him to eat dirt in an attempt to teach the boy humility. It didn't work – humility was never one of Norman's strong points.

Norman loved the wilderness that surrounded the numerous small towns in which he grew up. He learned to swim, fish, and run on rolling logs at an early age. Even traditionally quiet pursuits such as chasing butterflies became, for Norman, an adventure. Once, he and his brother Malcolm attempted to climb a cliff in search of a particularly good specimen. Halfway up, Norman ordered Malcolm to wait. As his frightened brother clung on, Norman scrambled the remaining distance and captured the butterfly. Then he helped Malcolm back down. At the bottom of the cliff he said: "There are two things about catching butterflies, Malcolm. First, there's the catching. Then there's the butterfly itself."

One winter, Norman showed his bravery. As everyone else fled to the shore, he rescued a boy who had fallen through the ice of a frozen river. Sometimes his bravery bordered on foolhardiness, however. On vacation when he was ten, Norman watched his father swim across Georgian Bay at Honey Harbour. The next day he attempted the feat himself and was saved from drowning only by his father's prompt arrival in a boat. But his narrow escape didn't slow Norman down. The following year he made it all the way across.

At home, life was equally interesting. Norman liked to move furniture and would indulge his nascent artistic tendencies by completely rearranging the contents of a room to suit his tastes. Norman grew up in the days before television and radio, so the family would play games in the evenings. One was a word game where each child was given a new word. The one who pronounced and spelled it correctly was given five cents. Norman usually won.

Throughout his early years, everyone assumed that Norman would grow up to be a surgeon, and many of his interests lay in that direction. One day, Elizabeth noticed an unpleasant smell wafting through the house. She investigated and eventually discovered Norman in the attic studiously boiling a cow's leg so that he could remove the flesh and add the clean bones to his collection.

Norman graduated from Owen Sound Collegiate in 1907 and promptly went to work as a lumberjack in the north woods of Ontario. A year in the Algoma camps strengthened Bethune, and he was to find this useful when, in January 1909, he took a teaching position at Edgely, just north of Toronto. In a single room, he taught grades one to eight to students who were often only a year or two younger than he was. At first he had discipline problems, and there were often lines of students awaiting the strap at the end of the day. Sometimes he even came to blows with his students. On one occasion, the boys in his class brought in an older man to fight their teacher. Drawing on boxing skills he had picked up in the lumber camps, Bethune won comfortably, and the discipline problems stopped.

In the summer of 1909, Norman collected the $269.00 owed him for his work at Edgely and prepared to attend the University of Toronto. He took Physiological and Biochemical Science courses but had trouble settling into the work. His best mark was a 62% in Natural Science, and he had to write supplemental examinations in French, German, and Latin. He was bored and didn't like the city life. After two years, he applied to return to teaching, but in a very different setting from Edgely.

Frontier College had been established in 1899 as a way to teach workers in remote railway, lumber, and mining camps. Students were given free accommodation in the camps but were expected to put in a full day's work before classes were held in the evening. It was a hard life, but Norman appeared to enjoy it. He spent the winter of 1911/12 with the Victoria Harbour Lumber Company at Whitefish on the shore of Georgian Bay. There is no record of Bethune getting into fights at this time, and he appears to have taken satisfaction in solving the diverse problems he was faced with. These problems ranged from fixing broken phonographs to setting a fractured tibia for a Polish worker.

The summer of 1912 saw Bethune travelling through Michigan and Minnesota before taking a job as reporter with the *Winnipeg Telegram* newspaper. Again the city life paled, and he applied to return to Frontier College and the simpler pleasures of the wilderness.

No positions were available, however, and in the fall Bethune was back at the University of Toronto. He seemed more settled this time around and, without the language commitments of the first year, his marks improved, averaging 69% in 1913 and 66% in 1914.

That year, Bethune was twenty-four, 5 feet 10½ inches (1.79 metres) tall, and had a chest expansion of thirty-eight inches (97 cm). His light brown hair already showed signs of receding, giving him a wide forehead above his blue eyes. He sported a thin moustache. He was physically fit from his work in the camps and had wide-ranging interests as a result of his varied experiences. He could paint, draw, and sculpt, and he was on the verge of his final year of medical training. But the world too, was on the verge.

On June 28, 1914, on his wedding anniversary, Franz Ferdinand, the heir to the Austrian throne, and his wife were assassinated by a Serbian student as they drove through Sarajevo in an open car. Austria declared war on Serbia; Russia declared war on Austria; Germany declared war on Russia; and France declared war on Germany. Nothing could stop the trains filled with enthusiastic young men that crossed the countries of Europe and headed for borders in response to plans for war made by old men years before. Britain was the only country that hesitated.

Monday, August 3, 1914 was a civic holiday in Ontario. It was also the last day of peace. In Toronto, ten thousand people filled the streets and wildly greeted every new development in Europe announced from the steps of the newspaper offices. They cheered, they beat drums, they waved flags. On August 4, Britain declared war on Germany, and Canada, as a Dominion of the British Empire, found herself embroiled in an adventure that would be like nothing anyone could possibly predict.

Young men, terrified that the war would be over before they could take part, flocked to join the army. They assumed they would go to Europe, see some excitement, and be home in time to regale family and friends with stirring tales around the Christmas fire. Norman Bethune was no different. On September 8 he went to Valcartier, Quebec, and enlisted in the Number Two Field Ambulance Medical Corps. His first real war had begun.

National Film Board of Canada

Royal Navy

National Film Board of Canada

Canadian Air Force

National Film Board of Canada

Canadian Army Medical Corps

Trying on different faces. Bethune samples all three
Canadian armed forces between 1914 and 1920.

3

The First World War

The blood-bespattered faces of the dead.

In the spring of 1915 the ancient town of Ypres was the last corner of Belgium that had not been over-run by the invading German armies. The town lay at the centre of an eight-mile-wide, six-mile-deep bulge into the German line, where their advance had been halted in the bitter fighting of the First Battle of Ypres in the fall and winter of the previous year. The north of the bulge was held by the French and Belgian armies, the south by British troops, and the centre by the First Canadian Division.

Bethune arrived in France in February, 1915. On the seventeenth of April, his unit moved into the line at Ypres. Bethune worked as a stretcher-bearer, probably around the town of Gravenstafel. At first there was little to do. The spring was warm and the front line was quiet. As the trees began to bud, birds sang and flowers bloomed in the gardens of the houses abandoned by the civilian population. Ypres itself, although badly damaged and filled with refugees, could still provide many amenities to a soldier who could escape there for a few hours. But this was soon to change.

Throughout April, patrols had been reporting odd clanking noises coming from the German trenches. After a local attack on Hill 60, south of the Canadian line, soldiers reported that they had encountered a strange smell. German prisoners told stories of a frightful new weapon being prepared. The reports were confusing and they were largely ignored.

The afternoon of April 22 was quiet. The sun was shining and from the German lines a gentle breeze blew over the "no man's land" between the opposing armies. Just before 5:00, observers noticed a yellowish-green cloud rise from the opposite trenches and drift towards them. Almost leisurely, the cloud drifted to the left. It narrowly missed the Canadian soldiers, but enveloped a French unit from Algeria. The cloud was chlorine gas, and its appearance marked the first use of chemical weapons in the war. The Algerians never had a chance. Gagging, coughing, and suffocating, they collapsed and died in the bottom of their trenches. A few, choking and frothing at the mouth, managed to flee, and they spread panic ahead of the cloud. Within minutes, a huge hole appeared in the Allied line and through it poured thousands of gas-masked German troops. The Second Battle of Ypres had begun.

On the right of the Canadian line, Bethune was not directly affected by the gas attack. Nevertheless, the German breakthrough caused chaos all along the front line. Panicking commanders threw reserves in to hold the line and to counterattack. Fortunately, the Germans were surprised by the success of the gas attack, and they were not prepared to exploit it to the full. But they recovered quickly. On April 24, they released gas against the Canadians.

Imagine you are a Canadian soldier at Ypres on that day in 1915. Chlorine gas reacts with water to form an acid that burns exposed skin, so the first thing you notice is that your eyes, mouth, and throat feel as if they are on fire. You have difficulty breathing and you vomit. If you breathe in too much, your lungs are damaged. They fill with fluid and you drown. Without a gas mask you are completely vulnerable. Your instinct is to huddle down and protect your stinging face, but that is a deadly choice. Chlorine gas is heavier than air. It collects in trench bottoms, dugouts, and shell holes – all the places soldiers of the First World War felt safe. In those places during a chlorine gas attack you will die a painful death by suffocation in a matter of a very few minutes. If you cover your nose and mouth with a piece of cloth – one of the first aid dressings all soldiers carry – you might be able either to escape from the trench or to survive until the gas blows past. You will still feel very sick, and you will have to fight off the enemy, who will be following the gas to try and kill you by other means. But you will be alive for the moment. Often that was the best a soldier could hope for.

On April 24 and 25, Bethune must have seen many gas cases. There was little he could do besides speed them back to safety away from the fighting. However, in the days since the introduction of gas, the Canadians had learned. If you wet the dressing before placing it over your nose, it worked better. Many believed that if you urinated on the dressing, it would neutralize the gas. In any case, if you could stand the feeling of suffocation and resist the urge to run or lie down, the gas passed quickly, and you were fit enough to fight the attackers. So, as well as gas victims, Bethune saw a large number of regular wounds as the Canadians fought to stop the German advance. In the bitter fighting of the last days of April, the 18,000 Canadians around Ypres suffered 5,975 casualties, over 4,000 of which were wounds.

The lot of a stretcher-bearer in battle was not an enviable one. First World War trenches were not dug in straight lines. If they were, the enemy would only need to capture a small section of trench in order to shoot along it for great distances in either direction. To prevent this, trenches were dug with corners – from the air they looked rather like the battlements of a medieval castle dug into the ground. This meant that during an attack the enemy had to fight hard to win each small section and that the blast from any bomb or shell was limited. Unfortunately for the stretcher-bearers, it also meant many corners to negotiate, corners so tight that two men carrying a six-foot stretcher could not go around them. Thus they had to lift the stretcher, with its heavy load of wounded soldier, completely above their heads as they turned the corner. It was unpleasant and gruelling work, but the alternative, travel above the ground, could only be undertaken with a degree of safety after they had left the front lines far behind.

What was Bethune's life like at Ypres? He and his comrades had the job of collecting the wounded from the Regimental Aid Post, where they were brought from the front line or no man's land, and carrying them back to the Advanced Dressing Station. There, casualties began the long, painful journey to a hospital in Britain. Two stretcher-bearers had to carry each wounded soldier, weighing seventy or eighty kilograms, for distances of a kilometre or more. Even without lifting around the trench corners, it was exhausting work. After a very short distance, Bethune's shoulders felt as if they were about to dislocate. His arms ached and his hands went numb. Every step was agony as pains shot through his thigh and calf muscles and as the blisters on his feet burst.

In addition to the physical torment, he had to continually force himself to walk slowly, upright, and fight the natural urge to lie down as machine-gun bullets passed overhead or shells exploded nearby. Bathed in sweat and shaking from the effort, he would eventually reach the Advanced Dressing Station and deposit his precious load. Then he had to turn around and do it all over again.

Stretcher-bearers saved countless lives in the First World War, but there were two problems they could not address. Serious wounds could not be properly treated until the soldier was removed to a hospital far from the battle. Initially, the speed of removal was no faster than a man could walk. Then, until the railway was reached, it would be at the pace of a horse-drawn or motorized ambulance negotiating the shell-cratered and clogged roads. It was a long process and many wounded soldiers did not survive it. The problem of speed was not solved until the introduction of large helicopters after the Second World War allowed casualties to be flown to hospital rapidly.

The other problem for the wounded of Bethune's day was shock. A soldier's comrades or a stretcher-bearer could administer first aid to ease pain, close the most obvious wounds, and immobilize broken limbs. However, bullets, shell fragments, and shrapnel all caused horrific damage, the shock of which, combined with the inevitable blood loss, was often enough to kill a soldier long before he could receive anything other than superficial treatment. One answer was to give the soldier a transfusion to replace the blood he had lost and give him the strength to survive the effects of shock and live long enough to have his wounds treated. Unfortunately, in 1915 the science of blood transfusion was still in its infancy, and there was no way to get blood close to the front lines where it would do most good.

Bethune must have seen many young soldiers die in his care. The horrors had their effect on him. In a letter from the front he wrote: "The slaughter has begun to appall me. I've begun to question whether it is worth it. Attached to the medical services, I see little of war's glory, and most of war's waste." He was aware of the reasons so many of the wounded died before they could get help, but he was a prisoner of the technology of his time. Nevertheless, the memory of the incredible waste of life around Ypres stayed with him and that memory was to have a profound effect on his work more than twenty years later. In fact, the rest of Bethune's professional life can be seen as a struggle to minimize useless waste of life and reduce the suffering of both soldiers and civilians.

The Second Battle of Ypres had an intense effect on another doctor who was working as Brigade Surgeon to the First Brigade Canadian Field Artillery within a few kilometres of where Bethune struggled with his stretchers. On May 3, as the battle drew to its close, the exhausted doctor sat outside his dressing station. He had just seen his close friend buried. On a sheet of paper he wrote down his feelings in the form of a fifteen-line poem. John McCrae didn't survive the war, but the images he put together to create "In Flanders Fields" have become a part of our collective memory of that time.

Bethune's experiences of trench warfare were brief. On April 29, a shrapnel shell exploded close by, and pieces of it went through the calf muscle of his left leg. He had the sort of wound many soldiers prayed for. It was a "blighty" wound, bad enough to get you removed from the front line and sent home ("blighty" was soldiers' slang for home), but not serious enough to threaten your life. Now Bethune made the journey he had helped send many others on: through the dressing stations, to the railhead, to the docks, and over to England on a hospital ship. Two days after he was wounded,

Bethune was in a hospital in Cambridge. He spent three months recovering and a further three months on duty in England before he returned to Canada.

The war was turning out to be a much larger enterprise than anyone had anticipated, and the need for doctors was urgent. Bethune was persuaded to return to university in Toronto to complete his medical degree in a special accelerated course. After his time in France, he took to pronouncing his name in the way of his far distant Norman ancestors, "Baytune." The nattily dressed young student developed a reputation as an individualist who was hard to really get to know. He often appeared to have other things on his mind and was known to have a strong interest in the welfare of his fellow man and to have socialist ideas.

In December, 1916, Bethune received the degree of Bachelor of Medicine from the University of Toronto. One of his classmates was Frederick Banting, who was to give hope to all diabetes sufferers and achieve fame as the co-discoverer of insulin.

Instead of returning to the trenches, Bethune went as a replacement doctor to a private practice in Stratford. One day in April, 1917, while he was in Toronto, a girl pinned a white feather on his coat. The white feather was the symbol of cowardice and it was given to young men not in uniform. The girl gave Bethune no chance to explain why he was not in uniform, but the incident influenced him strongly. Within a month he had joined the Canadian Navy as a Surgeon Lieutenant.

Reports on his time in the Navy show that he took a great interest in the welfare of both the officers and the men he served with. He also made a study of the medical conditions that affected the sailors.

The end of the war found Bethune back in hospital, this time for a hernia operation. With his demobilization in February 1919, he faced a problem. He had enjoyed the excitement of the war, but it had unsettled him. What could he do now to find the challenge that would satisfy his need for diversity and drama? The next few years of Bethune's life were an apparently unfocused search for that challenge.

The search began in the prestigious Hospital for Sick Children in London, where Bethune took a six-month internship in 1919. While he was there, Bethune worked very hard but he also put a lot of effort into enjoying himself. It seemed that he was trying to live life to the full and to get everything he could out of it. Confidently, he deliberately drew attention to himself. To some, he was a breath of fresh air; to his more critical colleagues, he was unconventional, careless, and slapdash; to all, he was refreshing and amusing.

Like many others at that time, Bethune seemed almost surprised that he and the world in general had survived the war. His hedonism was shared by a great many people who began to live life as if each day were their last. They did everything – work, play, travel – at a dead run, in order to experience as much of life as possible. A wealthy Englishwoman, who admired Bethune and financed much of his later medical training, supplied the money for the frantic lifestyle Bethune embraced. He spent the money with abandon, dressed flashily, hosted drinking parties amidst the art and anatomical models that filled his apartment, and travelled in Europe, buying and selling art. Through it all, his evangelical mother wrote regularly, reminding her son of the benefits of a life without sin, and encouraging him to go to church and read the Bible more.

When the wild six months in London ended, Bethune decided to return to Canada, where he worked as a replacement doctor for private practices in Stratford and Ingersoll. Small towns in Ontario were not the high life of bohemian London, and Bethune managed to raise a number of eyebrows. On one occasion, he mortified his date for the evening by escorting her to a dance wearing a light blue suit, red tie, and yellow shoes. He was also in the habit of driving the doctor's Model T Ford around the quiet town of Ingersoll at top speed.

But he gave parties for the children of his district and was a dedicated doctor who did fine work and was well liked by his patients. In fact, he was so well liked that when it was time for him to leave Stratford, some of the townspeople banded together and offered to support him financially if he would remain. Bethune declined.

Bethune's desire to help the needy had also developed by this time. He treated the poorest patient just as conscientiously as the richest. Once, when he visited a sick farmer, he found the man's wife distraught because there was no one to milk the cows. After performing his medical duties, Bethune took the milking pail, rolled up his sleeves, and attended to the cows. But he was still restless.

After his short spells in practice, in February 1920, Bethune joined the new Canadian Air Force as a

Flight Lieutenant in the medical service. He did some research into the causes of blackouts in pilots and was photographed in flying gear in front of a plane and above the handwritten caption "The Compleat Aviator, N. Bethune."

But the air force wasn't for him either. In October 1920, he was granted a leave and never returned. Instead, he travelled back to London, where he undertook a second internship at the West London Hospital before moving north to Edinburgh to train as a surgeon. On February 3, 1922, Bethune was elected a Fellow of the Royal College of Surgeons. He returned to London to work as Resident Surgical Officer back at the West London Hospital.

It was 1923 now, and Bethune had achieved a measure of success and a broad training as a doctor. He was thirty-three years old, experienced, charming, and full of life. The world was at his feet, but his life was about to take another of the strange twists that punctuated it and prevented Bethune settling into what most mortals would consider an orderly routine. In 1923, Norman Bethune got married.

Twice divorced but never bored. Frances Campbell Penney no longer has to look at Bethune through "half-closed eyes." ca. 1935.

4

Personal Wars

*Now I can make your life a misery, but I'll
never bore you.*
– Promise made by Bethune to
his bride on their wedding day.

Frances Campbell Penney was beautiful. In photographs, her features appear delicate and are dominated by large, soft eyes that stare out from beneath long lashes with an almost pleading intensity. Often the eyes seem on the verge of breaking into a smile. She was intelligent, but she exhuded an aura of innocence and unworldliness. She also had a lilting Scottish accent, and Bethune later claimed that he fell in love "at first sound." Whatever the reason, when Norman Bethune first laid eyes on the nineteen-year-old Frances in 1920, he fell head-over-heels in love. Bethune was not a man to do things by halves – his love was obsessive, and it lasted, through two marriages and divorces and countless separations, for the rest of his life.

For her part, the cultured yet shy Frances was overwhelmed by the brash confidence of Bethune. She was conservative and cautious. He was penniless. Her mother didn't approve. From the first moment she saw him, she knew Norman Bethune was the sort of man who would attract Frances, and she was scared he would sweep her daughter off her feet. She was right. That is exactly what happened.

Bethune courted Frances for three years. At last, she received a legacy from her uncle. The pair were married in a registry office in London on August 13, 1923. Without even waiting for the wedding photograph to be properly developed, Bethune whisked his new bride over to Europe for a honeymoon. The first his parents heard of the marriage was a telegram from the Channel Islands: "Married Honeymoon Here Very Happy Writing."

There is a medieval legend about a valiant knight who courted a fair lady. When he won her, she tested his bravery by throwing a rose into a lion's den and asking him to retrieve it. The knight entered the lion's den, rescued the rose and presented it to the lady. Then he mounted his horse and rode away alone. Her pointless gesture had shown a lack of trust and had killed the knight's love for her.

Frances knew the story of the knight and the lady, and it came rushing back to her one day shortly after she and Bethune were married. They were out walking and came to a deep ravine. It could be avoided and there was no reason to cross it, so Frances was horrified to hear her new husband say: "I dare you to jump it. I'd rather see you dead than refuse." Frances was brave. She jumped the ravine, but Bethune's irrational behaviour and need to dominate those around him put an unbearable strain on their relationship. Claiming not to understand his own behaviour, Bethune later apologized, but like the knight's for the lady, some of Frances's love for Norman was lost that day.

After they made up from the ravine incident, the pair embarked on a grand tour of Europe. They went to Switzerland to ski, Italy to visit galleries, Paris to wander around museums – and they spent money wildly. After several weeks in Vienna, where Bethune studied at the hospital, they were broke. With their last few pennies they wired for more. The money arrived and Bethune went out to collect it. When he returned, most of it was gone, spent on a small statue that had caught his fancy. In a fury, Frances smashed the statue. But the fight didn't last. By that evening, they were out in their finest clothes to spend what was left of the wired money.

They established a pattern: irrational behaviour by Bethune, anger from Frances, a quarrel, sometimes even a separation, then a reconciliation and a continuation of the high life. The emotional highs and lows must have been exhausting and confusing for Frances as Bethune seemed to be deliberately trying to make his wedding day prophesy come true.

Bethune had told Frances to always look at him through "half-closed eyes." But even that way, he must have been hard to live with. He likened himself to a butterfly that irrationally batters its wings against a light with no direction to its life or death.

When the money was almost exhausted, the couple returned to Canada, but Bethune was no closer to finding his life's purpose. He studied briefly at the Mayo Clinic, lived with his sister Janet in Stratford, and considered setting up a practice in Rouyn in northern Quebec. It was Detroit, with its noisy, vibrant growth that finally attracted him. In the winter of 1924/25, he opened an office beneath an apartment at 411 Seldon Avenue.

At first, patients were few and could often only pay in kind; a grocer supplied vegetables, a butcher meat, a hardware dealer a bed. The young couple could barely buy food, yet the apartment was hung with French Impressionist paintings and artworks bought in Europe. When they had no money, Frances and Norman quarrelled about it. When they had some, Norman spent it or gave it away, and they quarrelled about that. Frances disliked Detroit and America. The city was dirty and vulgar, and she saw it as uncivilized and decadent.

Frances could only stay home while Norman worked, and she was beginning to feel dominated by him. In 1925 she left him to visit a friend in Nova Scotia. Then she went to see her brother in California. Bethune wanted her back. He wrote that he still loved her desperately and missed her.

In 1926 she did return, but so did the quarrelling. Bethune was working hard. He had got himself a job teaching Prescription Writing at Detroit College of

Medicine and Surgery. He began his first lecture with: "This subject is a deadly bore but you must learn it and I must teach it to you." He adopted an exaggerated English accent and, as usual, was always immaculately dressed. He even affected carrying a cane, and wore old-fashioned wing collars, black tie, and gloves. He topped off this costume with a Homburg hat. However, Bethune was not above vulgarity, and one morning he explained his lateness with the statement: "Gentlemen, there is no relief like that of defecation."

His hospital work brought him contacts and some rich, paying clients, but he still went out in the middle of the night to see those who could not pay. He delivered the babies of Mexican workers and tended to the neighbourhood prostitutes. He became more and more angry at what he saw. He felt helpless when he watched a baby die and knew that a twenty-dollar-a-week job for the father would do more for the family than all his medical skills could. To Frances, he complained: "It's like putting a mustard plaster on a wooden leg. When they need treatment they either don't know it or are afraid they can't pay for it. When they finally do come, it's often too late, or their health has become completely undermined. And what can I do for a prostitute, when her problem is not really that she is diseased, but that she is a prostitute?"

He resented his colleagues, who charged outrageous sums for treating the wealthy yet would not go out at night to tend to the poor. And he took many of his frustrations out on Frances. It was too much. In the fall of 1926, she left him and returned to her family in Edinburgh.

At the same time, Bethune was diagnosed with pulmonary tuberculosis. He wrote "my dear girl don't worry or fuss. You can tell your people that I took your money, wasted it and left you stranded and, beyond calling you a fool for your action and I a knave for mine, what's to be said? You have done nothing wrong except to have consigned yourself and your money to a man who did not appreciate the one and was careless with the other."

Even when he was undergoing the long treatment for his illness, Bethune's relationship with Frances continued by mail. He wrote hoping that all her memories were not bitter and telling her that he still loved her even more than ever and that he wanted to see her again.

This time his pleas fell on deaf ears. Frances had had enough. In June 1927 she began divorce proceedings. The separation from Frances and the enforced inactivity of his treatment grated on Bethune's need for activity. The tension built up until, unwittingly, Frances gave him an outlet.

She wrote that a friend she had been seeing since the separation had ill-treated her. Bethune exploded. All his pent-up frustrations were violently released. Sick and almost penniless, he left hospital and travelled to Pittsburgh, where he bought a pistol and planned to kill Frances's friend. Bethune thought he was going to die of tuberculosis anyway, so he figured he had nothing to lose. He intended to turn himself in to the police after the murder.

Bethune invited the friend, a wealthy businessman, to his hotel room for a drink. There he pointed the pistol at him and announced his intention, but the man refused to defend himself. He invited Bethune to shoot and said, "I deserve it." Unable to shoot in cold blood, Bethune beat the man with the pistol. The sight of the unresisting man bleeding shocked Bethune into pity. He helped his victim to a chair and tended to his wounds. Then they got drunk together before Bethune helped him into a cab. Bethune returned to hospital with the bloodied hotel towel as a souvenir.

Even after the divorce was finalized, Bethune could not let Frances go. Obsessively he kept writing to her, even proposing that they remarry. If she was not prepared to do that, he desperately asked her to come to see him so they could meet, if only as friends. He blamed himself for her unhappiness and was glad that Frances was at least happier now that she was away from him.

His persistence had an effect, and Frances returned to Canada. Bethune was in better health and working successfully in Montreal, and for a brief moment it seemed things might work. Norman and Frances remarried on November 11, 1929. Then the quarrelling began again. Bethune was as irrational as always. On one occasion, Frances asked him to buy some meat for supper. When she returned home she found him sitting on the floor studying a skeleton.

"Did you remember the meat?" she asked.

"Yes," he replied distractedly, "it's in the refrigerator."

Frances opened the door. There, to her horror, was, not a roast for dinner, but a human intestine that Bethune had brought back from the hospital to study.

Eventually, Frances sought solace with Bethune's friend, A.R.E. Coleman. Bethune wrote from a lecture tour of the southern American states, "I love you and always will however much you may hurt or wound me.... I will not obtain a divorce."

A month later his mercurial temperament had reversed itself, "Well, my dear, the unexpected has happened as usual. I have fallen in love and want to marry this girl that I feel sure I can be happy with. It was love at first sight with both of us...let us give up trying to reconcile our irreconcilable natures...let us...live apart as friends."

Tactlessly, he went on to say, "You will love her. You are both much the same.... Will you write to her?"

Frances didn't write, and Bethune's new love affair died as suddenly as it had been born. But the relationship with Frances was doomed. After he returned, Bethune, Frances, and Coleman planned how to acquire the evidence of adultery required for divorce. After the divorce went through, the three went out and celebrated with champagne. During the celebration, Bethune told Coleman, "I don't give away my wife, I only lend her." Shortly after, Frances and Coleman were married.

Bethune realized that the collapse of his relationship with Frances was his fault. He was sorry for the unhappiness he had caused and likened himself to a gardener hacking clumsily at a tree in an attempt to mould it to his idea of how it should look.

He knew their relationship could never work and that to attempt a third time would damage them both. He determined to leave Frances alone. As he put it, "you and I must die to each other. Let us remember it only as a dream. Good-bye, my sweet Frances."

Nevertheless, they continued to see each other and write. They even had a doll which, like the living child of divorced parents, spent time alternately with each of them, at least until Bethune set his Montreal room on fire and the doll burned.

Bethune led the high life and met a lot of other women, two of whom he even proposed to, but none could match Frances in his affections. He always remained attached to her, and their failure to live together was one of the greatest disappointments of his turbulent life. But as he was losing his personal wars, Norman Bethune was chalking up extraordinary professional victories.

Plotting some escapade. Bethune and a fellow TB patient
at Trudeau Sanatorium, Saranac Lake, N.Y., 1927.

5

The War Against the White Plague

Lack of time and money kills more cases of pulmonary tuberculosis than lack of resistance to that disease. The poor man dies because he cannot afford to live.

There is a popular image of John Keats as the typical consumptive poet, languorously penning melancholy verse as he coughs delicately into a silk handkerchief. It is completely false.

Keats, Robert Louis Stevenson, Orwell, Chopin, Gauguin, Goethe, all died of "consumption," as tuberculosis (TB) used to be called, and there was nothing romantic about it. For months they suffered from fevers, weight loss, tiredness, and night sweats. Any physical exercise exhausted them and they could not work. As their lungs deteriorated, wracking fits of coughing brought up large amounts of bright arterial blood. Eventually, there was not enough lung left to absorb oxygen, and they died.

Evidence of tuberculosis has been found in the four-thousand-year-old, mummified bodies of Egyptian kings. Almost half a millennium before Christ, Hippocrates called consumption the most prevalent disease of his time. He recommended that his doctor colleagues not treat consumptive patients since the disease was invariably fatal, and the death of a patient was not good for a doctor's reputation.

In 1720, Benjamin Marten speculated that TB was caused by tiny living creatures, and that it could be transmitted from person to person through saliva. He was right, but a century later, TB was still the leading cause of death in the western world.

There seemed nothing anyone could do. *Mycobacterium tuberculosis* thrived in the overcrowded, unsanitary cities of the industrial revolution. It stalked the dark streets and ground its inevitable way through whole families. But by the beginning of the twentieth century there was some hope. Fresh air and complete rest appeared to help. All over Europe, sanatoriums grew up where patients could rest and, with luck, recover.

Of course, you had to be wealthy enough to afford the sanatorium. Many victims were so deeply involved in the struggle to earn enough money to feed their families that they did not seek help when the first subtle symptoms manifested themselves. By the time they sought medical care, most of the poor were too far gone for the rest cures to be any help at all.

This was the situation when Bethune, weakened and losing weight, began coughing up blood in the fall of 1926. He was diagnosed with pulmonary tuberculosis. His was a moderate case, and only in one lung, so the prognosis was for a full recovery. On December 16, after a short rest back at Gravenhurst, he entered the Trudeau Sanatorium on Saranac Lake, New York.

The Trudeau Sanatorium consisted of two infirmaries, a laboratory, nurses' residences, pavilions, therapy centre, library, chapel, post office, and twenty-eight cottages. Its staff of 200 looked after 160 patients, each of whom paid fifteen dollars a week for a six-month stay. The idea was that rest and fresh air would arrest the course of the disease, and the patients could then learn to live with it. The ability to remain inactive and learn to live with things was not a character trait Bethune possessed. As soon as he was allowed off complete bed rest, he fretted. Two strong elements of his personality came out.

Bethune always attempted to change things around him for what he saw as the better. Usually his attempts resulted in grandiose, and sometimes impractical, schemes. At Trudeau Sanatorium, he began making plans for a university on the site. For teachers, it would draw on the varied talents of the patients, and it would have moving walkways to transport patients between lectures so they could rest. The plan was rejected, but ten years after Bethune left, something very similar was set up – without the moving walkways. The closest Bethune came to realizing this particular dream was when he taught a course in Anatomy to the nurses. The course was well received, at least until the lecture on reproduction, which the administration cancelled as too explosive a topic for Bethune's entertaining but unconventional teaching methods.

Bethune also had a lifelong distrust of authority and power, which led him to break almost every rule he came across. Just because he was suffering from TB and in a sanatorium, he saw no reason to abide by rules he didn't agree with.

Smoking was not allowed.

Bethune gleefully had his photograph taken, sitting in a cane chair in the sanatorium lounge, ostentatiously smoking a cigarette.

The patients were to avoid all excitement.

Bethune organized parties supplied with wine smuggled in from Quebec.

Patients were only allowed passes out of the sanatorium three times a month.

Bethune stuffed clothes with blankets and pillows, left the fake figure on his bed, and sneaked out of the grounds to the local tavern or town whenever he felt like it.

Of course, Bethune was not the only one to break the rules, he just did it more openly and with more style than others.

The subdued atmosphere of Trudeau was shaken by this eccentric Canadian who drank tea from a silver service, wore a beret, used a long cigarette holder, and walked the halls tapping his cane on the floor. His sense of humour became well known. On one occasion, just after the Medical Director had turned down

Bethune's idea for a university, he threw a party, hired an orchestra, and invited prominent townspeople. In the midst of it all he made a formal presentation of a travelling bag to the Medical Director. The joke was not missed, but it was probably not appreciated.

But Bethune's life was not all a joke. In fact, it was in ruins. He had sold his Detroit practice, Frances was filing for a divorce, and his TB was not improving. His darker side came out in his attempt to kill Frances's friend. Bethune also discussed methods of suicide, his favourite of these being to take a dose of morphine and swim out into the lake. But his health was the one problem that he could do something about. He read everything he could find on tuberculosis. Eventually he came across a procedure called artificial pneumothorax, which he thought would help him. The procedure had first been proposed in the early nineteenth century when someone had noticed that consumptive soldiers with non-fatal bayonet wounds to the chest showed improvement in the disease. When the bayonet wound opened the area between the lung and chest wall, it allowed air in and partially collapsed the lung. This allowed the infected lung to rest and promoted healing.

Artificially producing this condition was a hit-and-miss affair until X-rays allowed some precision in the placement of the opening. In Bethune's day, the operation called for a needle to be inserted into the chest and for air to be allowed in naturally, or pumped in, until the diseased lung collapsed. The great advantage was that the patient could still function using the other lung. The appeal to Bethune must have been that this would allow him to both rest his lung and get back to his life.

With characteristic determination, Bethune worked on the sanatorium doctors. They refused to allow the procedure because it was dangerous, and they patiently explained all the risks. Theatrically, Bethune threw his shirt open, bared his chest, and declared, "Gentlemen, I welcome the risk!"

He won. On the morning of October 27, 1927, his infected lung was collapsed. As Bethune waited in his cottage to see if the procedure had been successful, he occupied himself in painting a mural on eighteen metres of paper that he plastered around the walls. Called, *The T.B.'s Progress, a Drama in One Act and Nine Painful Scenes*, it showed in illustrations and verse the course of Bethune's life and where he thought it would go in the future. Bethune portrayed himself as an infant being born, a knight in armour fighting off childhood illnesses, and a figure in despair being attacked by TB bats. The last scene showed Bethune in the arms of the Angel of Death beside a graveyard on whose tombstones were written the predicted dates of death of the artist and his friends at the sanatorium. Bethune chose 1932 as the time of his demise.

Bethune was wrong about when he was to die, but he was right about the collapsed lung – by early December he was already well enough to be discharged. He returned briefly to Detroit, where his colleagues assured him his successful practice was ready for him to take over. Bethune declined. He was no longer interested in success and making money; his first great cause, a major step towards that day on the

Malaga road, had taken hold of him and he felt an almost religious fervour.

Bethune thought it was criminal that such an obviously successful procedure as pneumothorax was not being used more. Thousands of curable patients were dying every year simply because most doctors were too conservative to try something new. It was unacceptable and he was going to do something about it. The first step was to become a thoracic (chest) surgeon specializing in the treatment of TB patients. What he needed was an expert in this new field to work with and learn from. Fortunately, there was such an expert close by, at the Royal Victoria Hospital in Montreal.

The Royal Victoria at that time was a Protestant, male-dominated, class-structured bastion. Things were done a certain way, and there could be no deviation from that way. Everyone was expected to know his or her proper place in the social and professional hierarchy. It was not the sort of institution someone of Bethune's character would be drawn to, but it was prestigious. Bethune was attracted by the opportunity to work under two well-known doctors: Dr. F.A.C. Scrimger, who had won the Victoria Cross for valour at Ypres in 1915, four days before Bethune himself had been wounded, and Dr. Edward Archibald. Archibald was the Canadian pioneer in the relatively new field of thoracic surgery. For someone who wanted to learn the field, he was the man to work with.

Bethune wrote and asked to work under Archibald, who agreed, on condition that Bethune take some basic training in biochemistry. This he did at Ray Brook Hospital, New York, and in April of 1928, he arrived in Montreal, ready to begin a new career at a time of life when most doctors are settling into comfortable, established practices.

During the First World War, as many Canadians succumbed at home to tuberculosis as died overseas in battle. In 1925, TB killed almost three thousand Quebecois – eight hundred in Montreal alone. Bethune was determined to change that, and he set about his task with vigour. For eight years, at the Royal Victoria Hospital and at Sacré-Cœur, he studied, experimented, researched, and operated with all his characteristic flair. The operating room staff at the Royal Victoria Hospital became used to sudden loud curses ringing out during Bethune's operations. Often the expletives were accompanied by loud clangs as surgical instruments that had displeased the outspoken surgeon flew across the room. The anger was focused, however. As often as not, he took the discarded instrument home, studied it, and improved on it. Within a week or two, a better version would be in use in the operating room. So successful were Bethune's modifications that a 1932 catalogue of medical supplies features a full page of his surgical instruments.

Most successful were the Rib Shearers, which are still in use today. Bethune was stumped as to how he could improve on the old ones until he went in to pick up a pair of shoes from repair. The instrument the cobbler was using to cut off old nails from shoes caught his attention. He bought it from the surprised man and had a modified version made from harder steel for use in his operations.

Bethune also developed an improved pneumothorax machine, which he used on himself. His left lung still required regular treatments to keep it collapsed, and these Bethune would administer himself. He would walk into the ward, undo his shirt, and, without anesthetic, insert the needle into his chest, pump in air from his own machine, and then continue with his work.

Bethune's work dominated his life, especially after his second divorce from Frances. He was incredibly focused on his goals and would stay up all night to work on a research problem or the design of a better surgical instrument. When he wasn't working, he was entertaining artists, poets, and anyone he found interesting at late-night parties in his flat. His drive and energy became legendary, but they made him enemies too. His lack of patience with those who thought more slowly than he did often led him to be rude and cruel. He hated mediocrity and would often deliberately make a fool of someone he disagreed with, expressing his hostility in ill-mannered and childish ways. Once, in a restaurant, he spotted someone he disliked. Excusing himself, he explained he had to go over and annoy the person.

As a surgeon, too, Bethune had his critics. He tended to select desperate cases to work on and to work very fast. This meant that many of his patients died, but on the other hand, many who would have died had he not operated, lived. More methodical surgeons, like Archibald, considered Bethune too flashy a surgeon and even dangerous in some of his techniques. Bethune was capable of criticizing himself as well. One extremely risky operation on a man no one else would operate on went wrong, and Bethune had to amputate the patient's leg. Despite the fact that no one held him responsible, Bethune insisted on standing up at the next staff meeting and describing the operation and what he saw as his own mistakes.

He cared deeply about his patients. When a dying girl he had been unable to save asked him to kiss her, he did so, even though she was highly infectious and he was running a risk by doing it. When asked why he had taken such a risk, he replied, "A doctor works with more than just medicine."

Once, his patient was a ten-year-old girl, the only child of a poor storekeeper. Her name was Yvette, and Bethune called her "my child." A year before, she would have been easy to cure – but not now. The family was poor and had delayed asking for help. When they did seek medical attention, doctors misdiagnosed and minimized the seriousness of her condition. Now, her entire right lung was abscessed. It was killing her. What could be done?

Bethune's colleagues shook their heads sadly. "There's nothing to be done," they said. But it was Bethune who would have to face the distraught parents who had brought their child to him for help. For Yvette to live, the infected lung would have to be removed. This was major surgery, and it had been done only a few times around the world. It had never been attempted in Canada, on a child. Yvette would proba-bly die. Then, Bethune would have to tell the parents that, despite his best intentions, he had killed her. Without having made up his mind, Bethune arranged for the operating room to be ready the next morning, just in case. Then he went home.

All night he lay awake and wondered what to do. Should he do nothing and give her a little more life before her inevitable death, or should he operate and run the high risk of killing her? At last, around 4:00 a.m., he came to a decision. His whole life had been centred around action and taking control. He hadn't been worried about the risks where his own health was concerned, and risk was an inevitable part of being alive. He would operate.

After a few hours' sleep, he arose, bought a doll for Yvette, and went to the hospital. Word had spread that something extraordinary was going to happen, and the viewing area of the operating room was packed. Some felt that they were coming to watch something closer to an autopsy than to surgery.

The operation was long, and it was often touch-and-go, but Yvette survived. Bethune was jubilant. That night he wrote to a friend:

> My child is well.
>
> It was a very beautiful operation.
>
> I felt very happy doing it.
>
> The entire right lung was removed – the first time this has been done – in a child of 10 in Canada and the 45th operation of its kind ever been done in the world. Isn't that nice?
>
> Yes, I will sleep deeply tonight.

Bethune was often unconventional in his treatments. One of his patients insisted that his stomach pains were the result of a frog he had eaten. The man obviously had a psychological problem, but nothing could change his mind. Bethune resolved to cure at least this manifestation. He acquired a frog and brought it to the hospital. After the patient had been given an enema, Bethune, unnoticed, slipped the frog into the toilet bowl. The patient's pain disappeared.

On another occasion, an old man came in with a massive infection around his right lung. Bethune was faced with a problem. The man had been operated on two years before, but the infection had recurred. To operate again would be extremely risky because, at his age, the patient would probably not be able to withstand the shock of major surgery. Bethune withdrew half a litre of pus from the man's chest and found it massively infected with streptococci and other bacteria. For a solution to his problem, Bethune went back to something that had been known since the sixteenth century. He opened the infected area and allowed as much pus as possible to drain for ten days. Then he placed a test tube full of live maggots into the hole and shone a light on them to drive them deep. Four days later, the maggots were dead and the infection less. Bethune washed the wound and repeated the process. Within two weeks the infection was gone and the wound healed, all without dangerous surgery. Bethune's flexibility and willingness to try something different had saved the man's life.

Today, tuberculosis still kills three million people worldwide every year. Rest cures and the surgical methods that Bethune promoted and used are, since the discovery of antibiotics, no longer applicable. Nevertheless, in Montreal during the thirties, Dr. Norman Bethune was at the forefront of the struggle against the disease, and countless people survived to have families and productive lives as a direct consequence of his drive and his unorthodox techniques.

Beneath walls crammed with modern art lies the scene of wild parties, intellectual debate, and children's art classes. Bethune's apartment in Montreal. ca. 1935.

6

The War Against Mediocrity

If I could only repress my irritating delight in shocking the timid, I think I might learn to be decent too.

Norman Bethune felt that most people lived a routine life, unaware of either their own potential or the world around them. This applied particularly to the wealthy, who were so focused on their material possessions that they knew or cared nothing for the rest of the world. He had little patience with people he saw as dull or unwilling to stretch themselves to the limit of their capacities.

At a dinner party given by a wealthy Montrealer, Bethune once tried to spark some controversy by ridiculing the passion for cleanliness and arguing that the natural odours of the human body should be allowed to develop. Bethune, who was generally fastidious in his own cleanliness and dress, was simply trying to get an interesting conversation going.

"How would we remain clean?" asked one horrified woman who did not realize that Bethune was talking for effect.

"Why, we would lick each other clean," Bethune told the shocked woman mischievously.

Another time, he arrived for dinner in the company of a prostitute whom he had obviously just invited in off the street. In front of the other horrified guests, he gave her a full meal and a drink. After she had finished, he announced: "Now, ladies and gentlemen, I shall return her whence she has come – the streets and degradation."

This behaviour was not calculated to make Bethune popular. Nor was his action when some guests arrived early for dinner at his apartment. Caught in the act of showering, Bethune answered the door completely naked and dripping water. The guests fled.

Understandably, Bethune upset and offended many people. However, those offended were most often people for whom Bethune had little regard in the first place. To his friends, he was extraordinarily generous. Each of his books had an insert which declared that it belonged to Norman Bethune and his friends. When someone complimented him on a wool overcoat he was wearing, he immediately took it off and offered it as a gift. A visitor to his apartment complimented him on the velvet drapes in his front room. Bethune took scissors, cut one side off, and presented it to the surprised woman He brushed aside her protestations by saying that he was only giving her something that she liked. His eccentric spontaneity, by turns delightful and infuriating, earned him both close friends and bitter enemies.

There was a showy, almost arrogant streak to Norman Bethune. He was a man of many natural talents and he assumed everyone was the same. He believed that anyone could do anything he or she wanted if they worked at it. To prove his point, he boasted that he could have one of his paintings hung in the Spring Exhibition at the Art Museum in Montreal. He went away and painted *Night Operating Theatre*. That spring it was exhibited.

But he could happily accept the opposite too. After he had spent weeks working long hours on a scientific paper on the physical signs of TB, he showed it to a friend. The friend criticized the paper. Bethune agreed and immediately tore it to shreds. Then he moved on to something else.

Bethune rarely stayed with one thing for long. He wrote short stories and poetry, but only occasionally, when a subject suggested itself strongly. He never worked consistently at developing one of his talents. There was always something different around the corner to snag his interest. When he took a course in painting, he showed up infrequently and worked independently. His artistic and literary endeavours were simply an expression of his restless spirit, which found many outlets.

To make a statement or point, Bethune often went out of his way to shock people. In the days when doctors were expected to dress very soberly, he once, in response to a dare, did his medical rounds at the hospital dressed as a lumberjack. On another occasion, he went to a party dressed in shoes, trousers, and overcoat, but without either a shirt or jacket. He had a yellow roadster, and, wearing a green hat and long scarf, he drove it around Montreal at high speed.

At times, he put himself at risk to make a point. One New Year's Eve, the conversation turned to the effect of cold on the human body. One of the guests stated categorically that no one could remain in the frigid water of the river outside for as long as a minute. Bethune derided the suggestion. Someone else agreed with the first speaker and wagered that it was not possible. Bethune stood up, walked out the door, and waded into the river, where he stayed immersed for a full minute. Then he returned and sat silently before the fire while his numbed body thawed out. Point proven.

He also used himself as a medical guinea pig. To prove that blood in the lungs was absorbed, he had someone introduce blood into his lungs while he slept. The next day when he was X-rayed he noted with satisfaction that no blood could be seen in his lungs.

Eventually, Bethune's odd behaviour became too much for the more conservative Dr. Archibald, and he was let go from the Royal Victoria Hospital in 1932. Now an internationally known chest surgeon, Bethune was offered the position of head of the new tubercular unit at Sacré-Cœur. With the grand title of "Chef du Service de chirurgie pulmonaire et de bronchoscopie," Bethune joked that he was going to get a tall white hat with "Chef" written on it. But he was very pleased. At last he was in charge of a department and could pursue his ideas without hindrance.

Despite his professional success, Bethune was chronically short of money, partly because he refused to charge his few private patients. He always maintained that if he were to have a private practice, he would not charge, but would put a donations box beside the door. It probably would have worked, too. After a fire in his apartment burned his clothes, he showed up for work in a threadbare suit and shoes with no soles, for he was unable to afford new ones. The anesthetist who worked with him went around to all Bethune's patients and asked for donations. He raised three hundred dollars. Bethune showed up the following day in a new suit, but again he was utterly broke. He had given the rest of the money to the poor children who took art lessons from him.

While being his own boss made his relations with his colleagues at Sacré-Cœur more conventional, he was still outspoken within the medical community. He gave frequent addresses at Canadian Medical Association conferences and was noted for being unorthodox and entertaining. One afternoon he spoke to the American Association of Thoracic Surgery. He had listened to a series of self-congratulatory speeches by the top people in his field. Each had emphasized how well things were progressing and how few people now died during chest surgery. Bethune stood up and tore into his colleagues for accepting only easy cases to make their statistics look good and refusing to work on the more risky ones even though lives could be saved by doing so. He made a lot of enemies that afternoon.

Shunned by the conservative establishment of his profession, Bethune moved more and more into artistic circles. He found that creative people tended to understand his own drives and impulses more readily, and his apartment was often a centre for the Montreal artistic community. A wide variety of people were commonly to be found there, discussing everything from politics to art. He kept one wall of his main room clear so that witticisms that came up in the course of these conversations could be written down.

When someone first came to Bethune's, they were ushered into the bathroom, where there were four cans of different coloured paint. The surprised guest was asked to select one, dip his or her hand in, and make a print on the wall. The guest's name was then written across the palm.

The parties were sometimes wild, fuelled by Bethune's tendencies to insult people. These tendencies were exacerbated when he drank, which he did often and to excess. He was at his least pleasant and most difficult at these times and got himself into many squabbles, which his friends had to bail him out of.

But Bethune's apartment was not used exclusively for partying. Three afternoons a week and Saturday mornings, his front room hosted the Montreal Children's Creative Art Centre. The art lessons were instructed by some of the top artists of the time, and all expenses were paid for by Bethune, sometimes with money collected by his anesthetist. There was no fee, and the children were encouraged to express themselves creatively. They were taken around to locations in the city and then provided with paint and paper and told to go ahead and paint. The sessions provided a welcome break from drudgery for the Depression-era children, and the open approach to learning was novel for its day. The school attracted attention, and the children's work was exhibited widely.

As the thirties progressed, Bethune's political position became more radical. As always, he was outspoken about it, but now the enemies he was making were a lot more sinister than offended socialites at dinner parties. One day he returned from the hospital to find his apartment had been broken into, his things destroyed, the paintings by his children ripped into shreds, and swastikas daubed on the walls. The police appeared disinterested, and Bethune doubted their investigation of the culprits would be pursued very vigorously.

The world was changing. Bethune, never one to stand back and let things happen, was being swept along with it towards causes much more sweeping and much more dangerous than those he had espoused before.

Gazing to the future. Bethune returns from the Soviet Union ready to take up the fight against fascism and for universal health care. 1935.

7

The War to Change the World

Let us take the profit, the private economic profit, out of Medicine, and purify our profession of rapacious individualism. Let us make it disgraceful to enrich ourselves at the expense of the miseries of our fellow men.

One afternoon, Bethune's car was caught in a traffic jam in Montreal. Seeing the crush of people on the sidewalk and assuming a bad accident had occurred, he went to see if he could help. What he found was not what he expected. Protesters were lined across the street. They carried banners demanding milk, bread, and jobs. In front of them, a line of mounted police advanced. As Bethune watched with rising horror, the police charged. The crowd broke and fled, but the police kept on, swinging wildly to left and right with their truncheons. People were staggering, bleeding, falling. Bethune saw one injured man callously thrown aside by a police motorbike.

When he returned to his car for his bag, Bethune found a bleeding, retching man sprawled on the hood. He helped the man into the back seat and began to patch his wounds. Surrounded by a chaos of sirens, shouts, screams, and horses' hooves, Bethune felt as if there was a war going on in his own town.

In fact, there was a sort of war going on, between the millions of Canadians thrown out of work and into poverty by the economic collapse of the Great Depression and the forces of authority who were unable or unwilling to do anything to help.

To many, it seemed that fascism, which had swept to power in Italy and Germany, was but a step away from taking over in Canada. One in every nine Canadians, a million people, needed some kind of federal relief just to keep from starving. Relief in Montreal meant one free meal a day at a soup kitchen. The meal consisted of weak soup, bread, a slice of sausage, and tea. Montreal also had shelters for the homeless, but these were so dirty and overcrowded that, in the summer, many people preferred to spend the night in the open in Fletcher's Field. There, every night, you could see hundreds of unemployed men sleeping as best they could under blankets of that day's newspapers. People were suffering, and the government was doing nothing to remedy the situation. The politicians seemed to care only about the businessmen who were paying workers starvation wages and living in comfort themselves.

When the unemployed complained, they were labelled "communists," and the police were used to break up any demonstrations. When the fascist and anti-Semitic thugs of Adrien Arcand's National Social Christian party took to the streets of Montreal to march or to smash the windows of Jewish-owned shops, the police stood by and watched. Even the Canadian Prime Minister, William Lyon Mackenzie King, was an admirer of Hitler and the way he was leading Germany. The man who was already stifling free speech and brutally persecuting Jews appeared to King to have "appealing and affectionate" eyes. The man who was about to plunge the world into war and launch the horrors of the Holocaust was sized up by the leader of the Canadian government as a philanthropist. People who did truly care about their fellow man were being forced into more and more radical positions.

Bethune cared. He cared passionately, but in an unfocused way. He would help anyone who needed it, happily puncture bloated egos, and speak out dramatically against any system he saw as adding to society's problems. But his instinctive distrust of any authority kept him from joining one of the many organizations that were working for change.

In the early years, Bethune's anti-authority position was taken, as often as not, simply to antagonize someone or to provoke a response. Emotionally, he tended to be radical, always going out of his way to help the underdog and those less fortunate than himself. Politically, he was conservative, being generally against socialism and trade union organizations.

What changed his mind was the realization that many of his patients were becoming sick or were dying because of their social position and not for medical reasons. The poor got sick and died. The rich got sick less often and recovered more often. So politics became a factor in Bethune's emotional concern for others.

In 1934, Bethune presented a case to the Canadian Progressive Club in Montreal. It concerned the imaginary John Bunyan, a poor worker living in a congested, dirty apartment building. In Bethune's hypothesis, based on what he had seen all around him, Bunyan is infected with TB by his aged mother, who lives with the family. The first doctor he goes to misses the diagnosis through ignorance of the symptoms. Eventually, a second doctor takes an X-ray and Bunyan is sent to a sanatorium. However, he is released too soon and returns home to infect his wife and children before dying.

Bethune asked his audience, "Who is responsible for Bunyan's death?"

Bethune answered his own question with a long list of culprits: the landlord for not improving the tenement, the first doctor for not knowing enough about the disease, the second doctor for not examining the rest of Bunyan's family, the sanatorium staff for releasing the patient too early, and the government for forcing a sick and infectious man to continue working and thus spread the disease.

Bethune went on to suggest a number of remedies: a publicity campaign to increase public awareness, better training of doctors in recognizing tuberculosis, X-rays of children, segregation of active TB cases, and the establishment of light industries where partly cured patients could work before being returned to society.

The suggestions were so revolutionary and far-reaching that they could be attempted only by the government. To make the government implement change would require political action. Bethune began by opening a free clinic, where he examined and treated women, children, and unemployed men.

But he was still conservative politically. At a Canadian Club luncheon in 1935 he had to be restrained from disrupting a speech praising the medical system in Soviet Russia. George Mooney, with whom Bethune worked at the free clinic, argued that Bethune could not properly judge the speaker's opinions without seeing what he was talking about first hand. That August, Bethune sold his car in order to pay for a trip to Russia to attend the International Physiological Congress. Bethune's old classmate from Toronto, the now famous Dr. Frederick Banting, was also at the Congress.

All through the thirties, Russia was a potent symbol for anyone with political thoughts. Either Russia represented the realization of a dangerous philosophy that destroyed the established order and threatened the stability of the world, or it was a dream made real, where the poor and the downtrodden had for once taken control from the rich exploiters. For the unemployed of the Depression, the communist experiment in Russia was a seductive dream. No one was yet aware of the mass murders Stalin was ordering in his prisons and camps or the orchestrated famines that were eliminating millions of unwelcome minority groups. You didn't have to be a communist to see Russia as a glimmer of hope in an otherwise hopeless world.

Bethune was in Russia for almost a month, and in that time he examined everything he could, from art galleries to medical practices. He didn't uncritically accept everything he was told, and he often got into arguments with his hosts, but overall he was impressed. The medical system in Russia was uncannily like the one he had been proposing as a replacement for the system that had killed John Bunyan. Workers received priority in the sanatoriums, which were lavish and free; children were routinely tested for TB; recovering patients were incorporated gradually back into the workforce. And the system worked. Despite the civil war and the years of chaos and isolation that had followed the revolution of 1917, the incidence of TB in Russia had been reduced by 50 per cent. It must have been extraordinarily gratifying for Bethune to see his ideas put into practice so successfully. He returned to Canada determined to spread the word about what he had seen.

His first opportunity came in December when he and three other Canadian doctors who had been to Russia were invited to talk about their experiences at the Montreal Medico-Chirurgical Society meeting. Bethune, who was the last speaker, was determined to balance whatever impression the others had given. He spoke eloquently, comparing the Russian experiment to a woman giving birth: a messy experience, but magical and full of promise for all that.

His strong support of the Russian system drove him even further away from his medical colleagues. Now he was more than an unorthodox doctor who challenged social customs. Now he was an unorthodox doctor who held radical – even dangerous – political views. He must have felt hopelessly isolated within his chosen profession. Characteristically, he responded through action.

The Montreal Group for the Security of the People's Health was a collection of health workers, social workers, and concerned lay people who came together under Bethune's leadership to try and change health care in Quebec and Canada. Throughout the winter of 1935/36, they researched health care in other countries and attempted to come up with a plan. They produced a report of almost four thousand carefully researched and argued words, that laid out a plan for state medical care. The group proposed salaries for doctors and nurses, health insurance, and care for the unemployed. In July, 1936, the report was sent to the Premier of Quebec, the leader of the Opposition, and more then fifty candidates in the upcoming provincial election. It had already been distributed throughout the medical profession.

Today Canadians take health care for granted. We don't think twice about going to a doctor if we're sick because we know the doctor will either treat us or pass us on to someone who will. No one is turned away from hospital doors because they are too poor. Doctors and nurses are salaried; there is health insurance; the unemployed are cared for. Bethune's suggestions are now the norm. The system may not be perfect, and, were he alive today, Bethune undoubtedly would have little difficulty finding a cause within the health care system that would benefit from one of his crusades. However, tremendous strides have been taken since 1936.

That summer, Bethune expected his report to stir up opposition. What crushed him was the indifference it met with. No one seemed to care about the situation, nor was anyone prepared to do anything about it. People feared that government involvement in health care was the first step on the road that led to Russian communism. Capitalism was proving inadequate to the task of caring for the people, yet few seemed to want anything to change.

Bethune argued his case at every opportunity. Even on a speaking tour to the ultra-conservative southern United States he created newspaper headlines by promoting government sponsored medical care. None of his efforts did any good. He became increasingly bitter and disillusioned.

His colleagues were increasingly turning away from him, too. In May of 1936, he had presented a paper outlining twenty-five mistakes he had made as a thoracic surgeon. It was an extremely useful exercise for young doctors, but in a profession that traditionally closed ranks when faced with criticism and tried to present a public aura of infallibility, the paper was bitterly resented.

Sometime during the winter of 1935/36, Bethune formally joined the Communist Party of Canada. It was a logical step as his political awareness grew. Over and over again, Bethune had seen proof that individuals could not bring about change on a large scale. Most recently, the reaction to his health care reforms had convinced him that only a strong organization could effect real change. So Bethune overcame his distrust of centralized authority and became a communist. At least the goals of the party were the same as his – to change the world for the better.

As Bethune rapidly became an outcast in his profession and his society, there was possibly even a danger that his well-known eccentricity might spill over into something more serious. A friend met him in a Montreal hotel in the summer of 1936. Bethune was wearing clothes that obviously had not been changed in a long time. He carried a small bag which contained only a phone book so that he could prove he had luggage when he signed in at the reception desk. Outside the hotel, his car refused to start. The gas gauge didn't work, so Bethune used a coat hanger to determine that the tank was bone dry. He had arrived on his last fumes of gas. He was living life on the edge. He had done all he could to change things in Montreal and Quebec and Canada. Nothing he did seemed to make any difference in the grand scheme of things. Could he go on doing the best he could as an individual? Bethune could not be satisfied with that.

An alternative presented itself that summer. Saturday, July 18, 1936 was hot in central Canada. The heat and humidity made concentration and work difficult. Into this lethargic atmosphere came electrifying news over the radio and in the late editions of the newspapers. A military coup was taking place in Spain. The army in the African Protectorate of Morocco was in revolt. They had slaughtered their opponents and declared a fascist state. In cities all across the Iberian Peninsula there was fighting in the streets as hastily armed workers threw up barricades and took on the army.

The news from Spain that July struck many people like a physical blow. This was it. At last the brutal face of fascism was being seen for what it was – cruel and aggressive. The Spanish people would not calmly sit back and watch their hard-won democracy be over-whelmed. Surely Canada and the rest of the free world would step in and help protect the legally elected democratic government of Spain against such an obvious threat? Surely they wouldn't let the fascists get away with this? Many hoped that the shots being fired on Spanish streets were the first in a war that would sweep fascism away for good.

It was a false hope. People overestimated the will of the Canadian government to act. They underestimated the support the fascists had in the boardrooms of big business and the corridors of power in Ottawa. Along with Britain, France, and the United States, the government of Canada did nothing. When Hitler and Mussolini openly supported the Spanish rebels with guns, planes, and troops, they did nothing. Even when British ships were bombed by Italian aircraft in the Mediterranean, they did nothing.

But there were individuals who were determined to do the right thing. Despite their own government's attempts to stop them, almost 1600 Canadians went to Spain to fight for the Republic. Some were communists, some were socialists, some were just working

men who saw a chance at last to do something. All saw
Spain as the place where fascism had to be stopped.
Almost half of the 1600 never came back.

Bethune could not ignore a cause like Spain. He
was a man of action and here was a perfect chance to
act. Here was a just cause he could contribute to, simply and without all the apathy, hypocrisy, and in-fight-
ing he had encountered when he tried to get things
done in Canada.

In August 1936 he was in a foul mood. Many of
his medical colleagues openly supported General
Francisco Franco, who was the leader of the army
revolt. The administration of Sacré-Cœur Hospital was
Catholic, and the Catholic Church supported the
rebellion. He put down his feelings in a poem called
"Red Moon."

> And this same pallid moon tonight,
> Which rides so quietly, clear and high,
> The mirror of our pale and troubled gaze,
> Raised to a cool Canadian sky,
>
> Above the shattered Spanish tops
> Last night, rose low and wild and red,
> Reflecting back from her illumined shield,
> The blood bespattered faces of the dead.
>
> To that pale disc we raise our clenched fists
> And to those nameless dead, our vows renew,
> "Comrades, who fought for freedom and the
>   future world.
> Who died for us, we will remember you."

In September, Bethune asked a friend to lend him two hundred dollars to get to Spain. The friend didn't have the money. Bethune approached the Canadian Red Cross Society – they rejected him. They had no plans to do anything for this cause. Then he saw an announcement that a Toronto organization was planning to send equipment to Spain and to establish a hospital there. He contacted them. They could offer nothing besides the return portion of a steamship ticket to Spain. He thought it over. He had had some good times in Montreal, but there was nothing left in the city for him. Spain was the place where the real problems of Bethune's time were being fought out, behind barricades in the streets and from hastily dug trenches in the hills. The very future of the world appeared to be hanging by a thread. Bethune's pondering was brief; there was really no choice.

He resigned his position at Sacré-Cœur, and on October 24, 1936, he boarded a ship for Spain.

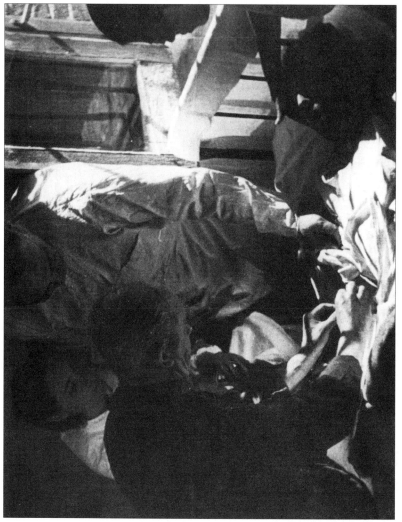

Performing the miracle. A blood transfusion to a wounded soldier in Spain. 1937.

National Archives of Canada

8

The War in Spain

*Madrid is the centre of gravity of the world
and I wouldn't be anywhere else.*

The large red crosses on the roof of the hospital in Guadalajara had been painted out – the fascist bomber pilots had been using them as aiming points. On the second floor of the building lay a wounded man. He was caked in dried blood, and old bandages covered the stumps where his hands used to be. Another bandage covered his now-useless eyes. The man could talk, but no one could understand what he was saying.

It was March of 1937, and many languages were being spoken in Spain. Tens of thousands of volunteers had flocked there to fight in the civil war that had grown out of the military coup of the previous summer. Germans, Italians, Britons, Frenchmen, Americans, Canadians, and a host of others had all come and been formed into the International Brigades. Bethune was running a blood transfusion service. That was why he was in this hospital with his Danish assistant Henning Sorenson when the doctor told him about the wounded man no one could understand.

While they were standing beside the bed, the wounded man said something. His words were unintelligible to Bethune, but Sorenson answered the man. "He's Swedish," Sorenson told Bethune, "No wonder they can't understand him."

While his assistant talked to the man, Bethune prepared the transfusion. Both the soldier's radial arteries had been torn and he had lost a lot of blood. His pulse was very weak. When the transfusion was over, the man smiled. His pulse was much stronger now. He spoke with Sorenson.

As they left, Bethune asked what the two had spoken about. Sorenson replied that the man had said that he had been home in Sweden only ten days before. He had arrived in Spain three days ago, and he had lost his eyes and his hands in his first battle. But what bothered the Swede most was that he could no longer be of any use either to his comrades or to the cause for which he had come to fight.

Bethune and Sorenson walked away in awe of the young man's bravery and dedication.

☙

Bravery and dedication were not in short supply in Spain in those days. Unfortunately, neither were brutality and barbarism. The passions unleashed by the rebellion in the summer of 1936 had been present for centuries. Romans, Visigoths, Moors, and Christians had all left their mark on Spain. Often considered only marginal to Europe, this was a complex land that few fully understood. A long, cruel war against the armies of Napoleon had given the world the word "guerrilla," but at the same time, Francisco Goya was producing some of the art world's great masterpieces. Spanish navigators had dramatically expanded knowledge of the world, but the conquistadors had conquered and destroyed the ancient civilizations of South America. The gold the conquistadors had brought back from the Americas had made the kings, the church, and the nobility unbelievably rich, but the peasants of Spain remained unbelievably poor.

Throughout the nineteenth century, and with almost religious fervour, the poor of Spain embraced any philosophy that promised them a better life. Communism, anarchism, and socialism all held sway in some region or other and each would burst violently to prominence periodically. It was said that the paving stones in Barcelona should be numbered in order to make it easier to replace them after they had been ripped up to form one of the frequent, hastily formed barricades.

In 1931 King Alfonso XIII was thrown out by popular demand, and a democracy was established. Elections were held and the government embarked on attempts to give the poor education, health care, and land. The army, the nobility, and the Catholic Church fiercely opposed these changes. There was frequent violence. In October of 1934, the miners in Asturias revolted against what they saw as the rise of fascism in the government. The Republic almost collapsed as the police and army, led by General Franco, resorted to brutal torture and mass killings in order to regain control.

Now, in 1936, Franco was leading his own rebellion. All the suppressed fear and hatred of past years came to the surface, and there were atrocities on both sides. The army and their fascist supporters carried out barbaric reprisals when they captured a town. A standard practice was to line the men up and force them to remove their shirts. A bruised shoulder was taken to mean that a rifle had been fired recently and was a certain death sentence. In Badajoz, thousands of people were herded at night into the local bullring and shot. The fascists were often anti-intellectual and went into battle shouting "Death to the Intelligence," and "Long live Death." One of their worst crimes was the cold-blooded murder of the famous poet Federico Garcia Lorca in a roadside ditch outside Granada.

But the violence was not all on one side. Resentment against the Church was common among the Republicans and, in some areas, led to the wholesale murder of priests and nuns and the burning of churches. Fascist prisoners were shot arbitrarily and as they gained power in 1937 and later, the communists were ruthless in suppressing those who disagreed with them.

As Franco's revolt grew into a protracted civil war, the many factions vied for power. In the north, around

Barcelona, the anarchists were strong, and they hurriedly set up communes, where money was eliminated and all the wealth was shared equally. In the city, all the businesses, from small cafés to heavy industrial plants, became co-operative ventures run by the workers. In Madrid and Valencia, the socialists and communists were stronger, and they established a more centralized government. Everywhere the people had to fight as the army moved out of the areas it controlled and attempted to conquer the entire country.

This was the situation that met the Swedish soldier that Bethune had treated in Guadalajara in March of 1937. It was the situation when Bethune had crossed the Atlantic and travelled to Madrid in October of the previous year. As the fascists gained strength on mainland Spain, Franco launched four columns of troops at Madrid, the Republican capital. Sure of a speedy victory, he counted on a fifth column of supporters to rise within the city and help him. It never happened. *Madrelinos* banded together as never before beneath the waves of German bombers trying to destroy their homes. In early November of 1936, as Franco's troops fought their way into Madrid's suburbs, the people flocked to stop them. They had no training and precious few weapons. Often soldiers had to wait until one of their comrades was killed or wounded in order to get their rifle. The two sides were so close that they sometimes occupied different floors of the same building, sending bombs and grenades up and down in the elevators at each other.

But help was on the way. The first international volunteers had been hastily organized and thrown in to the fight for Madrid. They were mostly Germans, Austrians, Poles, and Italians; many were veterans of the First World War; a lot of them had been hardened in Mussolini's prisons or Hitler's concentration camps. And they made a difference. Gradually the onslaught was stopped. Madrid did not fall and the war ground on.

Bethune came to Madrid on November 3, when the fighting for the city was just beginning. Suspicion and paranoia were running high. The workers were in charge and fighting for their lives. Working clothes had become almost a badge of loyalty. Bethune arrived dressed in a smart suit. His moustache helped give him an aristocratic or military look.

On his second day in the city, Bethune went to a hotel room to meet Sorenson, who had been sent ahead to prepare the way for the Canadian medical unit. They barely had time to shake hands before suspicious police burst in and grabbed a letter from Canada Bethune had just handed to Sorenson. The police were convinced that it contained secret, fascist orders. The letter began with "Darling," and the police officer became visibly embarrassed as he read through it. Flustered, he left, but Bethune took the precaution of shaving off his moustache and wearing overalls.

Despite the difficulties, Bethune was happy. This was where it was happening. This was where he wanted to be. He had arrived at the centre – but what was he to do? How could he be of most help? He had some medical supplies, some money collected in Canada, and his talent as a surgeon. He went around the improvised hospitals in town but found them to be adequately staffed. He went to Albacete, where the new International Brigades were being formed and trained, but found the French doctor in charge to be incompetent. In any case, Bethune did not have the temperament to work as just one member of a team under someone else. He had come to Spain to make a difference.

Bethune and Sorenson took the train to Valencia to purchase an ambulance for one of the Madrid hospitals. On the way, Bethune thought through an idea that had been forming in his mind as he toured around. Probably as a result of his experiences as a stretcher-bearer in 1915, Bethune knew how important it was to attend to the wounded rapidly. In particular, he knew how important speedy transfusions to combat shock and blood loss could be. Soldiers were dying in Madrid because the Spanish blood transfusion service was overloaded and poorly organized. The Republic had established a blood bank in Barcelona, but that was a long way from the front lines and many wounded never survived to get there.

Typically, Bethune saw the problem and saw the solution. First, he would organize a blood bank, and second, he would take the blood to the wounded, right into the front lines if necessary. It had never been done before, but that only increased the challenge. Bethune would be in charge of his own Canadian unit – good publicity for Canada, and for Norman Bethune.

Bethune was not an expert on blood transfusion, so he had to learn. He read everything he could lay hands on. Ancient Egyptian, Greek, and Roman manuscripts record attempts to transfuse many things –

including ale, wine, and animal blood – in bids to help the sick. The first recorded human blood transfusion occurred in 1492. In the same year as Christopher Columbus sighted the New World, the blood of three young men was given to the aged Pope Innocent VII in Rome. All three donors and the Pope died. In 1616, William Harvey announced that he had discovered how the blood circulated around the body. Half a century later, in Paris, Jean-Baptiste Denis treated an anaemic, fevered boy by giving him lamb's blood. His success was short-lived, and, as other of his patients died mysteriously, blood transfusions using animals were banned in France and remained so for 150 years.

The first successful human-to-human transfusion did not occur until the early nineteenth century, when James Blundell reawakened interest in England with his attempts to counter the frequently fatal loss of blood during childbirth. For generations blood transfusion remained a chancy business, and a great many people died in the process. In 1901 the reason for the deaths was revealed when Karl Landsteiner discovered that there are different types of blood. He labeled three different groups, A, B, and O. A fourth, AB, was added by another team of researchers the following year. If you mixed the blood groups, the patient receiving the transfusion would go into shock and perhaps die. It was not simple, but there was a pattern. AB patients were universal recipients and could accept blood from any of the other groups. O patients were universal donors and could give blood to any of the other groups.

The next advance was the discovery that adding sodium citrate to the blood would prevent clotting, and the blood could be stored and used later. This meant that donor and recipient no longer had to be physically joined during transfusion. The addition of dextrose to the blood and refrigeration both increased the length of time it could be stored. Apart from some rudimentary attempts to transfuse blood to wounded soldiers during the First World War, almost all the work had been done in the laboratories of large hospitals, not under fire in battle.

Norman Bethune didn't discover anything new about blood transfusions. His genius was to take existing knowledge and apply it to a different situation. In doing so, he saved lives.

Bethune and Sorenson flew to Paris, then to London to secure equipment. They purchased a station wagon in London for 175 pounds sterling and outfitted it with a kerosene- and gasoline-run refrigerator, sterilizer, and incubator. In all, they collected 1,375 separate pieces of equipment, including blood flasks, transfusion sets, surgical instruments, and lamps. The only problem they had was that the Canadian government, for political reasons, refused to give Bethune a letter stating that he was undertaking humanitarian aid, so that he would not have to pay duty crossing the French/Spanish border. Bethune paid the duty, but he long remembered with bitterness the obstructions placed in his way by his own government.

Back in Madrid, Bethune established the *Servicio Canadiense de Transfusion de Sangre* (Canadian Blood Transfusion Service) in the fifteen-room apartment of a German fascist diplomat who had fled the Republic. It was located in an upper-class neighbourhood, and consequently it was safe from the nightly attacks of the German bombers, which concentrated on the poor and working-class districts. Bethune worked with Sorenson and Hazen Sise, whom he had met in London, and he hired two Spanish medical students, a biologist, a technician, a cook, two maids, and a laundry man. By mid-December, the team had registered one thousand donors and had begun collecting and storing blood. Now he was ready to begin the real work – saving lives.

Driving at night through the pitch-dark streets of Madrid in December 1936 was eerie. The roads were deserted, and the rifle and machine-gun fire sounded very close. The destination was usually the improvised basement operating room of a hospital, but occasionally it was the front itself.

Casualty stations where the wounded received their first help typically were located very close to the fighting. One such was in a clump of trees within shouting distance of where the trenches snaked through the Casa del Campo park. On the night Bethune visited it, the only light was from the moon. By that dim light, Bethune, dressed in overalls with "Canada" and a red cross prominently displayed on them, quickly moved along the rows of wounded on the ground. He stopped beside a boy who appeared almost dead. He was in severe shock, his breathing was shallow, his eyes were sunken, and he was pale and unresponsive. Shells exploded nearby. Bullets whined through the air overhead. Carefully, Bethune found the vein in the boy's arm, exposed it, and inserted a tube that ran to a bottle of preserved blood. As Bethune opened a clamp, the blood began to flow into the boy.

Two bottles of blood – a litre – and the miracle happened. Colour returned to the wounded boy's cheeks, his teeth stopped chattering, and he opened his eyes and rose on one elbow to accept a cigarette. *"Gracias,"* he said. Now he would live long enough to have his wound attended to. It was a simple procedure, one that was repeated countless times in Madrid and during the battles in the hills around, but no one before Bethune had thought of it. It was his miracle.

Gradually the Canadian unit expanded. Bethune went to Marseilles and brought back the Renault truck. Then he went to the Malaga road.

☙

By the spring of 1937, the team had grown to twenty-five people, including hematologists, bacteriologists, doctors, nurses, and chauffeurs. They were supplying one hundred hospitals and casualty clearing stations for over one thousand kilometres of front lines. During battles, they gave up to one hundred transfusions each day. It was a stunning achievement in so short a time, but the situation was changing. Franco had been turned back in the suburbs of the capital, so he attempted to encircle the city. Bitter fights took place in the hills around Madrid as the noose closed inexorably. Franco was turned back again at the battle of Jarama, but only at great cost. Then the Republic enjoyed its first victory.

Mussolini insisted that his fifty thousand soldiers in Spain be given a glorious role. Franco agreed, and the Italians prepared. In early March they attacked down the main road to Guadalajara. At first their superiority in equipment and arms allowed them to advance rapidly. Then the Republic, led by the Italian volunteers of the International Brigades, counter-attacked. In the hills around Madrid, Italians bitterly fought against Italians. Mussolini's conscript soldiers were thrown back in disarray.

Bethune and his team rushed to the front, as close as they could get. Sometimes they got too close. As they drove around, they never knew if a machine gun would be facing them around the next corner. On one occasion, Bethune was driving a vehicle that came under fire. The occupants had to crawl back to the hospital along the ditch at the roadside. When they returned to the truck, they found a bullet hole through the windshield on the driver's side.

The danger and excitement thrilled Bethune. In the safety of Valencia, he complained that he had to get back to the front lines. For him, life and death were inextricably intertwined, and without being close to death, you were only half alive. He felt detached when he was at the front. "Every minute is beautiful because it may be the last and so it is enjoyed to the full."

Bethune was lucky at Guadalajara, but the strain was taking its toll on him. Even though he had an ability to sleep anywhere for a few minutes and awake refreshed, he was exhausted. But he wouldn't stop. He loved being in charge, he loved being needed, and he loved the excitement of danger.

The blood transfusion unit was working well. Bethune took pride in it and the fact that it was a Canadian achievement. He was happy, but he was already looking for new challenges. On a visit to Barcelona, he instigated the establishment of Canadian-funded orphanages for children of the war.

Around him, the war, too, was changing. More than the enthusiasm of the early days was needed in order to win. Organization was necessary, and the only people capable of supplying it were the communists. Authority began to extend its tentacles over the diverse organizations that had been hastily thrown together to get the Republic through the first months of crisis. One of these tentacles attempted to bring the Canadian unit under Spanish control. Bethune resisted fiercely, and a bitter fight broke out. To soothe ruffled Spanish feathers and to avoid embarrassment, the Canadian Communist Party suggested that Bethune return to Canada to take part in a speaking tour to raise money for arms for the Republic. On May 18, 1937, Bethune left Madrid. He had been as happy here as he had been anywhere else in his life. It had been a time ideally suited to his unique talents, and he had achieved great things. Times changed and he had to move on, but, having once experienced the heady intoxication of being in charge and making a real difference in a crisis, how would he take to being back in the staid atmosphere of Canada?

With a story to tell about the fight against fascism in Spain,
Bethune is welcomed back to Canada in 1937.

9

The War of Words

No one knows better than I the lure of pleasures, excitements, people...but those days are gone for me. I have steeled myself against them. The future looks lonely and dangerous.

It was only 8:00 in the morning, but over a thousand people were milling around Montreal's Bonaventure Station on June 16, 1937. As the train from Toronto pulled to a halt, the enthusiastic crowd broke through the barriers and flooded down the platform. They surrounded the well-dressed man who had just descended from a carriage. They lifted him shoulder high and carried him out to a waiting open car for a triumphal drive through the city streets. Bunting fell from open windows; people cheered and shouted; banners proclaimed support for republican Spain and opposition to fascism. Norman Bethune had come home.

Two days before, he had met the same reaction in Toronto. It must have done much to counter the mixed feelings with which he had left Spain after his conflict with the authorities. But the work was just beginning. That night, Bethune spoke to a capacity crowd of eight thousand in the Mount Royal Arena. Without notes and in a conversational tone, he described his experiences in Spain, the struggles of the Spanish people against fascism, and the need for money to support that struggle and to counteract the support Franco was receiving actively from Germany and Italy and passively from Britain, Canada, and the United States. He raised two thousand dollars.

Over the next three months he repeated his plea, sometimes twice a day, as he crisscrossed the continent. He talked of the Malaga road and the defense of Madrid; he berated his own government for not supporting his humanitarian work; and he warned that fascism was just around the corner in Canada.

Bethune was a spellbinding, charismatic speaker, whose passion could enthrall an audience. One fourteen-year-old boy came along out of curiosity and brought a dime to buy a milkshake. Instead, he gave Bethune the dime and retained his admiration for the man all his life. Another young listener remembered Bethune's words and felt twinges of conscience thirty years later when she went on holiday to Franco's Spain.

Sometimes he spoke in a small town to a mere handful of people, other times he spoke to thousands in Winnipeg, Vancouver, and Toronto. Donations varied depending on the political persuasion of the audience. Seven hundred people in Sudbury donated only $22.40. Three times that number donated eighteen hundred dollars in Winnipeg.

But the fundraising was not easy. It was difficult to convince people that what was happening in Spain had any relevance to a miner in Northern Ontario or a farmer in Saskatchewan. Bethune encountered the same lack of interest he had met when he presented his health care proposals.

Bethune saw the world situation as urgent. Only prompt, decisive action could stop Hitler's attempt to dominate Europe and Japan's to dominate Asia, but no one seemed in a hurry. The horrors of the Second World War would prove him right. Perhaps that war could have been avoided if the democracies had taken a firm stand in 1936 or 1937, but few were listening then. It was much easier to drift along, turn a blind eye, and hope that a repeat of the nightmare of the First World War could somehow be avoided. The frustration must have been unbearable for a man of action like Bethune. And there was another stress.

Bethune was a member of the Communist Party, but he was keeping it quiet so as not to scare off moderate supporters and undermine his work. Now he wanted to publicly declare his allegiance. Time and time again he sidestepped questions. Then in Winnipeg, at a banquet given in his honour at the St. Charles Hotel, he came clean. "I have the honour to be a communist," he declared. It was a weight off his shoulders, but it was another bridge irrevocably burned.

Now he could never return to the medical community in Canada. At his old hospital of Sacré-Cœur, the Mother Superior refused to meet him, thinking that she would be facing the devil if she did so. He finished his speaking tour in September, exhausted but strengthened. The war in Spain was going badly for the Republic and, in any case, the blood transfusion units were operating well without him and there were plenty of doctors. Returning to his former career in Canada was out of the question because of his political statements, and he probably no longer wanted to. World fascism was, to him, a disease just as virulent as the tuberculosis he had fought so long to eradicate, and it had to be fought just as ruthlessly. All the things that had been important in his life before – his partying, his art collection, his medical practices – were irrelevant. He was forty-seven. His personal life after Frances was empty. He had no children. His career was in ruins, and Canada could offer him nothing. Spain had toughened him, and what he had learned there had focused his view down to bare essentials. If fascism wasn't defeated, what else mattered? But the question arose, how could he make a worthwhile contribution? The answer was across the Pacific, where a new war was beginning.

In September, 1931, the Japanese had invaded Manchuria, driven out the Chinese, and created a puppet state. They had met little resistance, for General Chiang Kai-shek, the Chinese leader, was more concerned with fighting an internal war against Mao Tse-tung's[1] communist rebels than with fighting off the

1. Mao Tse-tung is now often spelled Mao Zedong.

Japanese. On July 7, 1937, while Bethune was in Timmins, Ontario, the Japanese struck again. This time, they launched a full-scale invasion of China itself. The attack was brutal as the invaders used terror as a way to subdue their enemy. When Nanking[1], the Chinese capital city, fell to the Japanese in December, 1937, they carried out a programme of systematic slaughter. They massacred as many as 350,000 people and raped 80,000 women.

In the face of such horror, Chiang Kai-shek at last formed a united front with Mao to oppose the invaders. At best, it was a shaky alliance, and the ruthless Japanese army swept the poorly trained, badly led, and inadequately equipped Chinese army before it, but at least someone was fighting back. Mao and his communist soldiers, hardened by years of war, fought a brutal guerrilla campaign in the vast, mountainous lands of North China. They controlled tens of thousands of square kilometres in which lived thirteen million people, but the battle lines were fluid. Movement was the key to avoiding a disastrous engagement against the superior Japanese forces.

To Bethune, it was Spain all over again, but not to most people. China was remote and mysterious. Goings-on there had even less relevance than what was happening in Europe. Even the Communist Party could do little; they were too heavily committed to the struggle in Spain.

Bethune saw the war in China differently. In his view it was a part of the same struggle against fascism

1. Nanking is now often spelled Nanjing.

and militarism, two evils that had to be defeated wherever they raised their heads. If the struggle was in the remote mountains of China, then that was where concerned people had to go.

Was this the cause Bethune sought? There was certainly the attraction of throwing himself wholeheartedly into an apparently straightforward struggle and hence avoiding the complexities that life back in Canada would bring. He read all he could find on Mao and the Chinese communists.

Bethune's friends were worried. China was not Spain. The areas the communists operated from were unbelievably remote and primitive by western standards. There were no roads, facilities, or medicines, and there was no help if anything went wrong. None of this stopped Bethune. He spent the fall of 1937 collecting money and organizing a team to go to China. By Christmas he had six thousand dollars, which he used to buy equipment for a complete hospital. Another doctor, Charles Parsons, and a nurse, Jean Ewen, had agreed to go with him. On New Year's Eve they had a farewell party in New York.

On January 8, 1938, the Canadian-American Mobile Medical Unit boarded the SS *Empress of Asia* in Vancouver for the nineteen-day trip to Hong Kong. Several friends felt that Bethune was lonely, that he had turned his back on everything in Canada, even that he was going to his death. But he had a cause – a cause that drew him on irresistibly, regardless of the cost. He was happy. Happier than he had been since the early days in Spain.

Wounded soldiers, malnourished civilians, and injured children –
all received Bethune's care in China. ca. 1938.

10

The War in China

Lord! I wish we had a radio and a hamburger sandwich.

On March 12, 1938, after he had been in China for less than two months, Canadian and American newspapers reported that Norman Bethune was dead. They were almost right.

All through February, Bethune had been forced to wait in Hong Kong and Hankow. Eventually, thoroughly frustrated with the slow Chinese bureaucracy, Bethune decided he would be most use serving with the communist Eighth Route Army. Parsons, with whom Bethune had already had a run-in over his drinking and possible squandering of funds, refused to accompany him and returned to the United States with what money was left. On February 22, Bethune and Jean Ewen headed north to Chin-kang K'u, the headquarters for one of the two areas controlled by the communists.

The journey was 1300 kilometres and Bethune expected it to take only a few days. It was to be four months before he finally rode into Chin-kang K'u.

Bethune's travel plans coincided with a major Japanese attack that cut the main railway north – the direct route to his destination. At the town of Lin Fen the small party met chaos. The Japanese were only a few kilometres away and advancing fast. The town was packed with panicked refugees and the rearguard of the retreating communist army. Bethune and Ewen scrambled aboard the last train back south. After a few kilometres, the train driver refused to continue on the heavily bombed line. The two Canadians joined an army unit escorting a mule train of forty-two carts loaded with desperately needed rice. The pace was slow, but at least they were heading away from the invaders.

They had only been travelling for a few hours along the dusty road when a cry from one of the soldiers announced that he had spotted the black shapes of two Japanese bombers. With only five old rifles between them, they could not fight back. The soldiers ran into the fields and took what cover they could. Like the German bombers in Spain, these came in low and unopposed. The bombs fell amongst the mule train, hurling pieces of metal and sharp fragments of rock everywhere. The bombs wounded several people and killed eighteen of the helpless mules. In keeping with the communist policy of paying for anything used by its army, the owners were paid one hundred Mexican dollars for each animal killed. When it was safe again, the rice was redistributed amongst the remaining carts, and the journey continued.

Bethune saw some unbelievable sights. At one point he noticed a young soldier ahead who seemed to be having trouble walking. When he caught up to him, Bethune was amazed to see that the boy had been shot through one lung. For a week he had been walking with this open, festering wound and the lung steadily filling with fluid. His heart was displaced by three inches (7.6 cm). There was little Bethune could do besides clean him up and put him on top of one of the rice carts.

Wherever they stopped, word spread that a doctor was there, and a ragged line of sick formed outside whatever hut Bethune was in. There was no chance to rest, only to move – one step ahead of the Japanese cavalry – and to treat the sick. Bethune noticed that in the near-deserted towns they passed through only two classes of people remained to face the invaders: the shopkeepers, who could not bear to abandon their possessions, and the beggars, who had no possessions and whose life could not get any worse regardless of who was in control.

On March third, in the city of Ho-chin, amidst the now familiar confusion of retreating soldiers and fleeing civilians, Norman Bethune celebrated his forty-eighth birthday by treating six wounded soldiers. He was beginning to notice that the only soldiers he saw had minor wounds to the arms and legs. The more serious cases with stomach, chest, or head wounds had long since died of infection and neglect. The day after his birthday he negotiated the ice floes to cross the Yellow River and was safe, for the moment, from the pursuing Japanese.

Gradually, Bethune and Ewen made their way west, attending to the sick and wounded as they went. On one occasion, Bethune was treating a child with convulsions when the mother, screaming the child's name, suddenly fled the cave they were in. The locals told the surprised doctor that she was calling back the child's soul, which had temporarily left his body.

As he saw more and more of the struggle in China, Bethune became increasingly bitter about Canada, the government, and his medical colleagues. He didn't regard himself as Canadian any more, but as a citizen of the world taking part in a revolution to change things for the better. He wrote, "I refuse to live in a world that spawns murder and corruption without raising my hand against them. I refuse to condone, by passivity, or by default, the wars which greedy men make against others." He was lonely and irritable. The only comfort he had was his certainty that he was right and that communism was the only way to achieve anything worthwhile.

In Sian[1] Bethune and Ewen met Dr. Richard Brown, a Canadian missionary who agreed to join their party for a few months, and received news that the medical supplies they had left in Hong Kong were on their way. On March 28, they set out north for Yenan.[2]

1. Sian is now often spelled Xi'an.
2. Yenan is now often spelled Yan'an.

Above Yenan there is an ancient pagoda which has come to symbolize Mao's resistance to both the Japanese and Chiang Kai-shek. In the early thirties, Chiang Kai-shek determined to exterminate the communists. He came close enough to his goal to force Mao and his 100,000 followers to set out on the Long March. They travelled for a year, fighting all the way, and covered over 9600 kilometres. Only a quarter of the marchers survived to establish a new base around the pagoda at Yenan. When Bethune arrived, it was still their headquarters, and it was here he met Mao Tsetung.

Two days after Bethune's arrival in Yenan, at 11:00 p.m., he was ushered into Mao's cave. By the light of a single candle, Mao, his tall figure dressed in a common soldier's uniform, stepped forward and greeted Bethune. As is the Chinese custom, they shook both hands. Then they settled down to talk.

The meeting lasted all night, and the conversation covered a wide range of topics, from the medical situation to Bethune's experiences in Spain and his plans to establish a hospital in the communist-controlled area. The two men got on well and Bethune was elated for days afterwards. Finally, he had met one of the leaders of the world revolution he had dedicated his life to.

In Yenan, Bethune was established in a cave cut into the soft soil. Beds were called *k'angs* and consisted of straw spread on top of a clay-brick oven in which a fire could be built for warmth. Bethune also acquired a helper, to cook, run messages, and tidy for him. At first, the seventeen-year-old boy was terrified of the tall foreigner, but Bethune showed him what to do and Ho

Tzu-hsin stayed by his side until the end. Bethune even taught Ho how to boil an egg just the way he liked it. It was a struggle, but when Ho succeeded, Bethune had their picture taken to commemorate the occasion.

After three weeks in Yenan, Bethune finally set off northeast for Chin-kang K'u, his original destination of so long ago. Instead of the direct route he had originally planned, Bethune was now on the last leg of a huge sweep through north China. But he was to be sidetracked once again. At the town of Sung-yen K'ou, he decided to build a hospital.

Brown accompanied Bethune to Sung-yen K'ou, but after a few weeks he had to return to his other duties. Jean Ewen remained as Head Nurse in the hospital in Yenan. Neither was to see Bethune again. Now he was truly cut adrift.

The aim of Bethune's model hospital at Sung-yen K'ou was to establish a facility where the wounded could recuperate and where doctors and nurses could be trained before being sent out to work at the front. The problem was that in a guerrilla war the front lines are continually shifting. A fixed facility is subject to attack. Bethune was warned of this, but, as with all the projects he called his own, he could not be dissuaded. The hospital was built.

The hospital worked during the weeks of its construction. One day, as Bethune operated on a soldier, the man lost a lot of blood. Bethune asked the nurses who would volunteer to give blood to save the man's life. No one did. They were afraid of the unknown. Men who would happily risk death fighting the Japanese were terrified of giving 300 cc of blood.

Angrily, Bethune berated them. It made no difference. Quickly he rolled up his own sleeve, took the blood, and transferred it to the patient.

A few weeks later some casualties arrived. One of the men was not seriously wounded but appeared dead. He was pale, cold, and motionless. Bethune recognized the symptoms from his experiences in Spain. Theatrically, he called all the local villagers out into the dusty square. Explaining the process of blood transfusion, he once more took his own blood and gave it to the soldier. As the villagers watched in awe, Bethune's miracle happened again. The apparently dead man quivered, groaned, opened his eyes, smiled, and looked about. Bethune never had any more trouble finding blood donors.

The model hospital opened on September 15, 1938, amidst celebrations, speeches, banners, and incongruous anti-fascist posters Bethune had brought from Spain. Bethune talked at length about the duties of doctors and nurses and the importance of proper sanitary techniques. He was justifiably proud of the hospital, which had been built in only five weeks. It boasted an operating theatre, sanitation department, playing fields for recovering patients, cookhouse, games hall, lecture room, and medical school. Since there were no textbooks, Bethune wrote one, the first-ever handbook of medical practices in guerrilla warfare. Unfortunately, those who had warned Bethune about building a permanent hospital in this kind of war were correct. Three weeks after the opening ceremony, Sung-yen K'ou fell to the Japanese and the hospital was destroyed.

The destruction of his dream taught Bethune a lesson. From then on, he concentrated on mobile medical facilities that could be set up wherever they were needed and rapidly moved whenever they were threatened. He designed a complete operating theatre that could be carried by three mules over the roughest mountain track and set up in a peasant's hut or a Buddhist temple close to the fighting. His watchword to the doctors was: "Go to the wounded. Don't wait for the wounded to come to you."

The mobile medical facilities were successful, but it was gruelling work. When Bethune heard of a battle, he would lead his team as close as possible to the fighting. Often they had to travel over a very harsh, mountainous landscape and, in winter, through deep snow. As soon as the operating room was set up, Bethune and his two Chinese doctors began work. The wounded were brought in by stretcher and were operated on immediately. The survival rate skyrocketed and the incidence of infection plummeted.

During an attack at the end of November, 1938, Bethune and his assistants operated on seventy-one soldiers in forty hours. As he worked, a few kilometres away other men poured machine-gun fire and hurled grenades amongst a milling mass of Japanese troops who had been caught in an ambush. Men screamed and ran everywhere through a hellish scene lit by the fires of burning trucks and tanks. When the time came to charge and finish off the enemy, the soldiers ran down the hillside, shouting, "If we are wounded, we have Pai-ch'iu-en to treat us. Attack."

"Pai-ch'iu-en" was the closest the Chinese could come to pronouncing Bethune, and the name was quickly acquiring a magical tone. The foreign doctor who had come to help the Chinese in their struggle was becoming a legend.

On another occasion, as Japanese shells whined overhead and exploded all around the Buddhist temple where Bethune had set up a temporary hospital, the team performed 115 operations in sixty-nine hours, a remarkable feat of endurance. At one point, Bethune noticed that the man in charge of the hospital was hovering at his shoulder. "Why are you here?" he asked. The man explained that if a shell killed the famous foreign doctor he would be blamed – correctly he thought – for not taking him to safety. Realizing that it was hopeless to argue with Bethune, the man was at least determined to stay so close to him that, if the worst happened, no one could accuse him of being somewhere safe while his charge was in danger.

After fifty-nine hours of continuous work they ran out of anesthetic. The next patient was tied down to the table with rope, and Bethune began cutting into his thigh. Fortunately, the man soon fainted from the pain. For ten hours, Bethune operated on fifteen patients who, until they passed out, could feel every cut of his scalpel and probe as he searched for shrapnel. It was finally over only when the enemy was defeated within two kilometres of Bethune's hospital. When he staggered, exhausted, out of the operating room, the village around him was a smoking ruin.

Not all Bethune's work was with soldiers. In one village, he amazed everyone by successfully operating on a boy's harelip, a procedure completely unknown to the peasants.

The gentleness and concern he had shown in treating tuberculosis patients in Montreal was also present in China. He used to take his own soup ration into the hospital wards. He would sit on a bed and ask a patient how he was doing. When the man opened his mouth to answer, Bethune would feed him a spoonful of soup. Once, when Bethune was leaving a hospital in a remote village, he noticed that the bottom step was missing. Jumping over it, he asked the attendant following him if he minded jumping. The attendant said "No." Bethune then asked if he thought the convalescing soldiers minded jumping. The villagers found a stone and the step was fixed.

But he was a harsh critic, too, and his famous temper had not been left behind in Canada. He would arrive at a remote hospital late at night, brush off offers of food or a bed, and immediately begin his inspection of the wounded. Any laxity in sanitary techniques or care of the wounded brought down his wrath.

At the village of Ho Chien Tsun, after ten hours of non-stop winter travel over the mountains, Bethune refused food and went to see the wounded. Conditions were bad. One soldier had an infected broken leg beneath bandages that had not been changed in a long time. In a rage, Bethune demanded, "Who is responsible for this?" When a Doctor Fong stepped forward sheepishly, Bethune castigated him mercilessly. He was incompetent, a disgrace to the medical profession, a danger to the brave soldiers who were risking their lives in battle, and the cause of this young soldier losing his leg.

Bethune did not care that losing face was the worst thing that could happen to the man, all he saw was incompetence and a poor doctor. Dismissing Fong, Bethune immediately prepared to operate on the soldier.

As he worked on the infected leg with its pieces of bone exposed, his anger grew.

Why was the leg not splinted?

There were no splints.

Why were splints not made? Did the soldiers stop fighting when they had no rifle? No! They went and killed a Japanese soldier and took his rifle.

Why was he being handed a carpenter's saw to cut through the soldier's bone?

It was the only saw there was.

Grimly, Bethune set about his work. A doctor's responsibility was to care for the sick. At Ho Chien Tsun, Doctor Fong had failed. He would have to be punished.

After two hours' sleep, Bethune and his party set off for the next hospital. On the way, his interpreter told Bethune Fong's story. In reality, he had no medical training. He was only a poor peasant who had grown up attending to the village water buffalo. One day the Eighth Route Army had passed through his village and he had joined. He began as a guard. In his spare time he taught himself to read and write, so he was made a nurse. He worked hard and became a head nurse. Night after night, he worked to learn the Latin names used by the doctors around him. By watching the surgeons, he learned the rudiments of medicine. There was no one else, so Fong became a surgeon. In Ho Chien Tsun he had been studying a few words of

English so that he could learn from the famous foreign doctor who was coming to his village.

Bethune was silent. He had not been fair to Fong. The man had shown incredible dedication to come as far as he had, and Bethune had made him lose face before everyone.

When the team returned to Ho Chien Tsun, Bethune searched out Fong, apologized, encouraged him to continue learning, and offered to let him join his team as an assistant. He did, and a year later, Fong was one of the doctors singled out to receive some of Bethune's surgical instruments when he knew he was dying.

The rigorous life was taking its toll on Bethune. He was thin and tired, and he looked ten years older than he was. He was completely deaf in one ear, his teeth were rotten, and he needed new eyeglasses. Hard work, loneliness, and an unvaried diet of millet or rice, potatoes, vegetables, eggs, and tea were all wearing him down. He wrote to a friend that he had not seen an English-language newspaper in six months and didn't know who the President of America or the Prime Minister of Britain were. He never learned more than a few words of Chinese and pleaded in his letters for books and magazines in English to ease his isolation. He never received any. At times it seemed to him that the life of hardship in China was similar to the rough life he had led as a youth in the logging camps of Northern Ontario.

To John Barnwell, with whom he had shared a cottage in the sanatorium at Saranac so many years before, he wrote that he missed someone to talk to. "You know how fond I am of talking! I don't mind the conventional hardships – heat and bitter cold, dirt, lice, unvaried unfamiliar food, walking in the mountains, no stoves, beds, or baths. I find I can get along and operate as well in a dirty Buddhist temple with a 20 foot high statue of the impassive-faced god staring over my shoulder, as in a modern operating room with running water, nice green glazed walls, electric lamps and a thousand other accessories."

Later in the same letter he listed the things he missed most: "I dream of coffee, of rare roast beef, of apple pie and ice cream. Mirages of heavenly food. Books – are books still being written? Is music still being played? Do you dance, drink beer, look at pictures? What do clean white sheets in a soft bed feel like? Do women still love to be loved?"

He also missed the money and supplies that he had been promised in Canada and America. Nothing was getting through, either because it was not being sent or because it was being intercepted on the way. He felt betrayed by the people at home.

By the late summer of 1939, the mobile units were working well. What was needed was a central training facility in a secure area, where nurses and doctors could be trained to go out to the front and tend to the wounded. It was the model hospital idea once more, but with more thought behind it this time. The hospital could be built again. What was needed was the money and equipment to run it. These had been promised but had never arrived. The only way to get them was to go back to Canada.

For the winter of 1939/40, Bethune planned a speaking tour similar to the one he had made upon his return from Spain. With the money he raised, he would buy the equipment and return to China in the summer of 1940. Of course, unbeknownst to Bethune, the world war against fascism had finally begun in September of 1939. It was too late to save the Spanish Republic – that had been finally crushed by Franco and his allies and had surrendered unconditionally on April 1 of that year – but belatedly the western democracies were saying "Enough!" to Hitler and Mussolini.

Ironically, Russia, which had led the struggle against fascism throughout the thirties, had betrayed her admirers by signing a non-aggression pact with Hitler in August of 1939, a cynical move that bought time before Hitler's tanks moved east in June 1941. Japan and China were still being ignored, and America would not become involved until the Japanese bombers appeared out of a clear Sunday-morning sky over Pearl Harbor two years down the road.

Bethune knew none of this in October 1939 when he was planning his trip back to Canada. He would never learn it. Throughout October he travelled on one last inspection tour. When the Japanese launched their tanks and soldiers against the communists late in the month, fierce fighting broke out everywhere. Bethune hurried to the front. On October 28 he cut his finger while operating on the soldier with the broken leg. As the world sank into war, Norman Bethune fought his last battle, an unwinnable one against the tiny bacteria that were poisoning his blood.

Beneath the only foreign flag the Chinese could find –the Stars and Stripes – Bethune lies in state while 10,000 mourners file past, Chu-ch'eng, China, 1940.

Epilogue

Remembrance of Wars Past

I am deeply grieved over his death. Now we are all commemorating him, which shows how profoundly his spirit inspires everyone.
Mao Tse-tung
December 21, 1939

If you had been a wounded American soldier in Vietnam, you would have stood a very good chance, despite the remoteness of much of the fighting, of having your wound treated faster than any soldier had in any previous war. Entire surgical units, complete with all necessary equipment and established in trailers similar to the portables behind many schools, were slung beneath giant Sikorsky Skycrane helicopters and flown as close as possible to the fighting. Politically, Norman Bethune would have been supporting the other side, but he would have approved of the principle of taking the doctors to the wounded rather than the wounded to the doctors. That was his philosophy, and he was the first to put it systematically into effect. In doing so, he saved countless lives in Spain and China and laid the foundations for future army medical units, which saved countless more.

Of course, the best way to save lives is not to have wars at all, but sometimes they are unavoidable. Bethune believed that his wars were necessary – essential, in fact, to improve the lot of his fellows and stop the spread of fascism. History has proved him correct.

Tuberculosis is not the killer it used to be, although the war is not completely won, and worldwide, millions still die each year of the disease. Universal health care, along the lines proposed by Bethune, is now sponsored by the government and is the right of every Canadian. Finally the fascists went too far even for William Lyon Mackenzie King and the other western leaders, and the world was convulsed by the Second World War. The fifty-five million dead of that conflict dwarfed the mere hundreds of thousands who died in Bethune's wars in the 1930s, when, with some determination, fascism might have been stopped relatively easily.

But being right does not mean that you will be recognized for it. People do not like to be reminded that they were wrong or were too slow to act. Bethune embraced the only political philosophy that seemed to be striving for the same goals he was – communism. In the Cold War of the 1950s and 1960s, it was not fashionable to make heroes out of communists, even when they were right. In addition, some of the things Bethune fought against did not change. Capitalism, which he saw as the root cause of much of the injustice and evil he struggled against, survived the Great Depression and the Second World War to emerge stronger than ever. Bethune would probably not have liked the path communism took, but, equally, he would have continued to speak out loudly against a system that put financial wealth and material possessions above the well-being of people.

In his homeland, Norman Bethune and his achievements were largely ignored for a quarter century after his death. He was remembered mainly by those who knew him and who shared his ideals. In 1952, his biography, *The Scalpel, the Sword: the Story of Doctor Norman Bethune* was published. In 1964, the National Film Board made a controversial film on Bethune's life. Because the film publicized a communist, the American government asked Canada not to distribute it in the United States.

In the early 1970s, Canada was trying to build up trade relations with China. It was a communist country, ruled by Mao Tse-tung, the man Bethune had sat up all night talking with in 1938, but it was a potentially huge market for Canadian goods. Canadians were surprised to discover that one of their own was regarded as a hero by millions of Chinese people. All of a sudden, Bethune's name became known. He became an instant hero. Books were written about him, films were made, and the house where he was born in Gravenhurst was preserved and turned into a museum. Cynics would say that the final irony was that Bethune's memory was being manipulated in order to open trade doors in China for a capitalist government that a living Bethune would have harshly criticized. In any case, the publicity brought Bethune's name and achievements to the attention of many more Canadians.

In China, they had always known what an extraordinary man Norman Bethune was. When he died, they carried his body through the mountains for four days. In January, 1940, it was moved again to Chu-ch'eng, where the body, draped in the only foreign flag the Chinese could find – the Stars and Stripes – was laid in state. Ten thousand people, many weeping, filed silently past to pay their last respects.

The villagers built a tomb for Bethune, carrying tons of marble through the Japanese lines to do so. It was an impressive structure with a large statue and carved quotations from people who knew him. When a Japanese advance threatened the town late in the year, the villagers removed the body and the statue and hid them. The Japanese used the tomb for target practice and destroyed it. When they were driven away, the villagers rebuilt the tomb.

In 1952, after both the Japanese and Chiang Kai-shek had been defeated, Bethune's body was moved one last time – to a park built to commemorate all those who had died in the struggle to rid China of the Japanese and to establish a communist country. Bethune's tomb and statue are prominent, and across the road is the large Norman Bethune International Peace Hospital. Hundreds of thousands of people visit the park each year.

Today in China, Bethune is still revered by hundreds of millions of people. Even in Canada, he is considered of "national historic significance." Were he alive today, the first fact would please him. The second, he would probably find amusing because it makes him sound like a ruined castle. He would laugh, and he would point out that the things he fought for were not just dry footnotes in history books. They were real causes, which affected the lives and deaths of thousands of real people. Then he would leave, to become a thorn in the side of complacency and indifference, and to remind governments that it is the people they govern who are important and not self-interest or the pursuit of power for its own sake.

The world has changed a lot since Bethune struggled to decide who to help amongst the exhausted refugees on the Malaga road. But that is no excuse for complacency. Were he alive today, Dr. Norman Bethune would find just as much injustice, just as many causes to support, and just as many battles to fight as he did when the enemies were tuberculosis and fascism.

THE END

Long before he was remembered in Canada, Bethune was almost worshipped in China. A memorial to the man and his work, probably in Chu-ch'eng, 1940.

Chronology of Norman Bethune (1890-1939)

Compiled by Lynne Bowen

BETHUNE AND HIS TIMES	CANADA AND THE WORLD
	1492 First recorded blood transfusion given to Pope Innocent VII – he and all three donors die.
	1616 William Harvey discovers the blood circulatory system of the body.
	1720 Benjamin Marten speculates that tuberculosis (TB) is caused by tiny living creatures and transmitted through saliva.
1772 Reverend John Bethune (Bethune's great-great-grandfather) leaves the Isle of Skye for the American colonies.	

BETHUNE AND HIS TIMES	**CANADA AND THE WORLD**

1775
Rev. Bethune is imprisoned during the Revolutionary War for loyalty to the British Crown.

1775
American Revolutionary War begins.

1776
American Declaration of Independence.

1783
After his release from American prison, Rev. Bethune flees to Montreal, where he establishes the city's first Presbyterian congregation.

1783
American Revolutionary War ends; United Empire Loyalists leave the United States (U.S.) to settle in Canada.

1882
Robert Koch discovers the tubercle bacillus and demonstrates its role in causing TB.

1890
Henry Norman Bethune is born March 3 at Gravenhurst, Ontario, to Malcolm Nicholson Bethune and Elizabeth Ann Goodwin Bethune.

1891
Sir John A. Macdonald, Canada's first Prime Minister, dies in Ottawa.

1892
Bethune's grandfather, also Dr. Norman Bethune, dies penniless in a home for incurables in Toronto.

1893
Bethune family moves to Beaverton, Ontario.

BETHUNE AND HIS TIMES	CANADA AND THE WORLD
	1895
	Wilhelm Roentgen discovers X-rays, which will lead to their use in the diagnosis of TB forty years later.
	Louis Pasteur, discoverer of micro-organisms and the germ theory of disease, dies.
	1896
	Wilfrid Laurier becomes Canada's first Prime Minister of French ancestry.
1897-1900	
Bethune family moves around Ontario to Toronto, Aylmer, and Blind River.	
1898	
Bethune asks to be called Norman instead of Henry.	
	1899
	The establishment of Frontier College allows workers in Canada's remote railway, lumber, and mining camps to receive an education.
	1900
	Mortality rate for TB in Canada is 180 per 100,000.
	Boxer Rising in China against Westerners; ends in 1901.

BETHUNE AND HIS TIMES	**CANADA AND THE WORLD**
1901 Frances Campbell Penney (Bethune's future wife) is born.	**1901** Karl Landsteiner discovers blood types O, A, and B and so explains the high mortality rate from blood transfusions.
	1902 Anglo-Japanese Treaty recognizes the independence of China and Korea.
	Researchers discover blood type AB.
1903-07 Bethune attends secondary school at Sault Ste. Marie and Owen Sound, Ontario.	
	1905 In Canada, Alberta and Saskatchewan become provinces.
	In Russia, the first parliament is created and the first workers' soviet; Czar Nicholas II's "October Manifesto" establishes reforms.
	Sun Yat-sen, Cantonese revolutionary, founds union of secret societies to expel Manchu dynasty, which had ruled China since 1644.
1907 Bethune graduates from Owen Sound Collegiate; goes to the north woods of Ontario as a lumberjack in the Algoma camps.	**1907** Sun Yat-sen announces the program of his Chinese Democratic Republic.
	Rasputin gains influence in the court of Russian Czar Nicholas II.

BETHUNE AND HIS TIMES

CANADA AND THE WORLD

1908
Dowager Empress of China, Tzu-Hsi, who has ruled China as regent since 1862, dies.

1909
Bethune takes a teaching position at Edgely (north of Toronto) from January to June then goes to the University of Toronto (U of T) to study Physiology and Biochemical Science for two years.

1911
Bethune works as a labourer-teacher under the auspices of Frontier College at Victoria Harbour Lumber Company, Whitefish, Georgian Bay, Ontario.

1911
Revolution in central China; Republic proclaimed; Sun Yat-sen elected president; appoints Chiang Kai-shek military adviser.

Robert Borden succeeds Wilfrid Laurier as Prime Minister of Canada.

1912
During the summer, Bethune travels through Michigan and Minnesota and then becomes a reporter for the *Winnipeg Telegram*.

Bethune returns to U of T in the fall to study medicine.

1912
SS *Titanic* sinks.

Norman Bethune

BETHUNE AND HIS TIMES	CANADA AND THE WORLD
1914	**1914** On June 28, Franz Ferdinand, heir to the Austrian throne, is assassinated in Sarajevo, touching off the chain of events that leads to World War I (WWI).
Bethune enlists as a private soldier in Number Two Field Ambulance Medical Corps in Valcartier, Quebec on September 8.	Britain declares war on Germany on August 4; Canada is automatically at war; young Canadians flock to join the army.
1915 Bethune arrives in France as a stretcher-bearer; his unit moves into the line with the First Canadian Division at Ypres, Belgium.	**1915** Second Battle of Ypres begins in Belgium; Germans use chlorine gas for the first time on a French unit on April 22; First Canadian Division in the centre of Allied lines gassed on April 24; Canadian Dr. John McCrae writes "In Flanders Fields" on May 3; Canadians suffer 5,975 casualties.
Bethune receives "blighty" wound – shrapnel in his left calf – on April 29; by May 5 Bethune is in hospital in Cambridge, England, where he stays for nearly three months.	
In November, Bethune returns to Canada and U of T's accelerated medical program.	
1916 Bethune receives Bachelor of Medicine degree in December; begins private practice in Stratford, Ontario.	**1916** Frederick Banting (co-discoverer of insulin) graduates in same class as Bethune.
	Blood for transfusion is refrigerated for the first time.

BETHUNE AND HIS TIMES

1917
Bethune relieves two physicians in private practice in Stratford.

As the result of being pinned with a white feather (symbol of cowardice), Bethune joins the Royal Navy as a Surgeon-Lieutenant in May; serves fourteen months on aircraft carrier, HMS *Pegasus*.

1918
Bethune has hernia repair in November.

CANADA AND THE WORLD

1917
Canadian forces responsible for a major Allied victory at Vimy Ridge in France in April.

Military Service Act imposes conscription and divides Canadians along French/English lines; to ensure the election of the incumbent Union Government, army nurses and female relatives of servicemen are allowed to vote.

October (Bolshevik) Revolution in Russia deposes the monarchy; Lenin becomes President of Council of Peoples' Commissars.

1918
Dr. John McCrae dies of pneumonia.

Allies and Germany sign Armistice on November 11, ending WWI.

Number of Canadians dying of TB equals number who died in WWI in battle (60,000).

Worldwide influenza epidemic kills 22 million people in two years.

BETHUNE AND HIS TIMES

1919

Bethune is demobilized and begins a six-month internship at the Great Ormond Street Hospital for Sick Children in London, England; combines hard work with a wild lifestyle; returns to Canada to work as a replacement doctor in Stratford and Ingersoll, Ontario.

1920

Bethune joins the new Canadian Air Force as a Flight-Lieutenant in the medical service in February; is granted leave in October and returns to London, England for twelve months' surgical training at the West London Hospital and then to the Royal Infirmary in Edinburgh.

Bethune meets Frances Penney.

CANADA AND THE WORLD

1919

Treaty of Versailles sets terms of post-WWI peace; League of Nations set up to ensure it.

In Canada, massive unemployment and inflation, the success of the Bolshevik Revolution, the rise of revolutionary industrial unionism (including the One Big Union), give rise to labour unrest in Canada and, most notably, the Winnipeg General Strike.

1920

Canada joins the League of Nations.

Arthur Meighen succeeds Robert Borden as Prime Minister of Canada.

End of civil war in Russia.

Adolf Hitler, an obscure Austrian politician, announces his 25-point program in Munich.

1921

William Lyon Mackenzie King succeeds Arthur Meighen as Prime Minister of Canada.

Eduardo Dato, Spanish Prime Minister, assassinated.

Communist Party of Canada founded as a secret organization in Guelph, Ontario.

BETHUNE AND HIS TIMES	CANADA AND THE WORLD
1922	**1922**
Bethune elected a Fellow of the Royal College of Surgeons and returns to London for eighteen months as a Resident Surgical Officer.	Benito Mussolini and his Italian fascists march on Rome and form the government.
	Union of Soviet Socialist Republics (U.S.S.R.) formed from the former Russian empire.
	Communist Party of Canada becomes an open party and changes name to Workers' Party.
1923	**1923**
Bethune marries Frances Penney on August 13 in London, England; they spend six months travelling in Europe.	Frederick Banting (classmate of Bethune's) wins Nobel Prize for discovering insulin.
	Hitler's "Beer Hall Putsch" fails in Munich, Germany.
	Canadian Air Force designated as "Royal."
	1924
	In U.S.S.R., Lenin dies; Josef Stalin struggles with Leon Trotsky for power.
1925	**1925**
After brief period of study at the Mayo Clinic in Rochester, Minnesota, Bethune opens an office in Detroit.	In Canada, TB kills 3000 Quebecois, 800 in Montreal area alone.
	In China, Sun Yat-sen dies.
Frances leaves Bethune.	In Germany, Hitler publishes volume 1 of *Mein Kampf*.

BETHUNE AND HIS TIMES

1926

Frances returns to Bethune but leaves again within the year to return to her family in Edinburgh.

Bethune teaches Prescription Writing at Detroit College of Medicine and Surgery.

Bethune is diagnosed with TB; treatment is begun at Calydor Sanatorium, Gravenhurst, and continues at Trudeau Sanatorium, Saranac Lake, New York.

1927

Frances begins divorce proceedings in June; Bethune receives news of divorce on October 24.

Bethune convinces doctors to collapse his infected lung using artificial pneumothorax on October 27; his lung heals quickly and he is discharged from the sanitorium in December.

CANADA AND THE WORLD

1926

Arthur Meighen succeeds William Lyon Mackenzie King as Prime Minister of Canada for three months and then is himself succeeded by Mackenzie King.

BETHUNE AND HIS TIMES	CANADA AND THE WORLD
1928	**1928**
Bethune receives training in laboratory research at Ray Brook, New York, from January to March.	Josef Stalin wins a power struggle to become leader of the U.S.S.R.
In April, Bethune goes to Montreal to train for four years as a thoracic surgeon at the Royal Victoria Hospital, where he often uses unconventional methods of treatment.	Members of the Communist Party of Canada are ordered by the Third International of the Communist Party to start their own trade unions; Canadian communists set up the Workers' Unity League to co-ordinate union activities.
	Chiang Kai-shek is elected President of China.
	In Britain, Alexander Fleming discovers penicillin and suggests possibilities for the treatment of disease.
1929	**1929**
Frances returns to Montreal and remarries Bethune on November 11.	Black Friday (October 28); American stock exchange collapses; Great Depression begins and lasts ten years.
	Kellogg-Briand Pact outlawing war signed by sixty-five states.
1931	**1931**
Catalogue of medical supplies features full page of Bethune's modified surgical instruments; in the fall Bethune visits sanatoria and lectures in the American Southwest.	Richard (R.B.) Bennett succeeds William Lyon Mackenzie King as Prime Minister of Canada.
	King Alfonso XIII of Spain deposed; democratic government of the Republic installed.
	Japanese invade Manchuria, drive out the Chinese, and create a puppet state.

BETHUNE AND HIS TIMES

1932

Bethune is acting head, thoracic surgery, at Herman Kiefler Hospital, Detroit for six months.

Bethune is let go from Royal Victoria Hospital.

Frances sues for divorce a second time and marries A.R.E. Coleman.

1933

In January, Bethune is appointed Chief of Pulmonary Surgery and Bronchoscopy at *l'Hôpital du Sacré-Cœur* in Cartierville, near Montreal.

1934

Bethune presents hypothetical case to the Canadian Progressive Club in Montreal and suggests remedies for society's social ills.

Bethune opens a free clinic.

CANADA AND THE WORLD

1932

Nazi party wins majority in German Reichstag elections.

1933

In Canada, the Co-operative Commonwealth Federation (CCF), a political coalition of progressive, socialist, and labour forces under the leadership of J.S. Woodsworth, meets for the first time. The CCF will become the New Democratic Party (NDP) in 1961.

Adolf Hitler is appointed German chancellor.

Franklin Delano Roosevelt becomes President of the U.S.

Japan withdraws from the League of Nations.

1934

In Canada, Mitchell Hepburn becomes Premier of Ontario with promises of reform; Dionne quintuplets born in Corbeil, Ontario.

Josef Stalin begins purge of the Communist Party in the U.S.S.R.

BETHUNE AND HIS TIMES

1935

Bethune tries to disrupt a speech praising the medical system in Soviet Russia.

In June, Bethune is elected to Council of American Association of Cardiac Surgery.

In August, Bethune goes to Leningrad and Moscow for the International Physiological Congress.

In November, Bethune joins the Communist Party of Canada.

In December, Bethune speaks glowingly about Soviet medicine at Montreal Medico-Chirurgical Society.

CANADA AND THE WORLD

1935

Incidence of TB in Russia has been reduced by 50 per cent since the Bolshevik Revolution.

In Canada, Workers' Unity League disbands and Communist Party workers are encouraged to become part of the mainstream union movement.

On to Ottawa Trek of unemployed men across Canada is stopped in Regina by the RCMP; riot leaves one dead and hundreds injured.

Mackenzie King succeeds R.B. Bennett as Prime Minster of Canada.

Nazis repudiate the Treaty of Versailles.

Despite having signed a twenty-year treaty of friendship in 1928, Mussolini invades Abyssinia.

BETHUNE AND HIS TIMES

1936

Bethune assumes leadership of The Montreal Group for the Security of the People's Health, which aims to change health care in Quebec and Canada; plan for state medical care is sent to politicians during Quebec election campaign but meets with indifference.

Bethune forms the Children's Art School of Montreal; writes poem "Red Moon" in August.

On October 24, Bethune sails for Spain and arrives November 3.

With Canadians Henning Sorensen and Hazen Sise, American Celia Greenspan, and Spanish personnel, Bethune establishes the *Servicio Canadiense de Transfusion de Sangre* (Canadian Blood Transfusion Service) in Madrid and begins saving lives with transfusions at casualty stations.

CANADA AND THE WORLD

1936

Supported by Hitler and Mussolini, General Franco leads fascist rebellion against the Republic of Spain.

George V, King of England, dies and is succeeded by his son, Edward VIII, who later abdicates in favour of his brother, George VI.

Maurice Duplessis and his *Union Nationale* party gain power in Quebec.

Battle of Madrid; international volunteers make first appearance fighting for the communist-supported Republic in November; Republican government moves to Valencia for the remainder of the war.

Chiang Kai-shek declares war on Japan.

BETHUNE AND HIS TIMES	CANADA AND THE WORLD
1937	**1937**
Bethune treats the Swedish soldier in Guadalajara; Spanish Ministry of War takes over the transfusion unit; Bethune starts Canadian-funded orphanages for children of the war.	Spanish rebels take Malaga, destroy Guernica.
	Hepburn re-elected in Ontario for his opposition to American industrial unionism.
Bethune returns to Canada on May 18; arrives in Canada to a hero's welcome on June 14 in Toronto and June 16 in Montreal; spends the summer on a cross-Canada lecture tour to raise money for arms for the Republic and warn people about fascism; in Winnipeg he admits he is a communist, thus isolating himself from the Canadian medical community.	Amelia Earhart disappears on flight over Pacific Ocean.
	In France, the Duke of Windsor marries Wallis Simpson.
In the fall, Bethune organizes the Canadian-American Mobile Medical Unit to go to China; farewell party held in New York on December 31.	Canadian volunteers in Spain are brought together in the Mackenzie-Papineau Battalion.
	Japanese invade China on July 7; massacre 350,000 at fall of Nanking[1]; Chiang Kai-shek forms reluctant alliance with Mao Tse-tung[2], communist rebel leader.

---

1. Nanking is now often spelled Nanjing.
2. Mao Tse-tung is now often spelled Mao Zedong.

BETHUNE AND HIS TIMES	**CANADA AND THE WORLD**

1938

On January 8, medical unit (Bethune, Dr. C.H. Parsons, and nurse Jean Ewen) boards SS *Empress of China* in Vancouver to sail for Hong Kong; on February 22, Bethune and Ewen begin four-month-long journey to Chin-kang K'u, a communist headquarters; in March Bethune meets Mao Tse-tung at Yenan[1].

On September 15, Bethune opens a hospital at Sung-yen K'ou; hospital is destroyed in October by Japanese; Bethune realizes he has to concentrate on mobile medical facilities.

1938

Japanese install Chinese puppet government in Nanking and withdraw from League of Nations.

In Spain, Franco begins offensive in Catalonia.

Canadian and American newspapers mistakenly report death of Bethune.

---

1. Yenan is now often spelled Yan'an.

BETHUNE AND HIS TIMES	CANADA AND THE WORLD
1939	**1939**
	Spanish Republic surrenders to Franco in April.
	Communist leader Stalin confounds the world by signing a nonaggression pact with fascist Adolf Hitler in June.
In late summer, with mobile units working well, Bethune plans to go back to Canada to raise money; medical school and model hospital opened in September at Nin-Yen K'ou.	Spanish Civil War ends; Britain and France recognize Franco's government; Spain leaves League of Nations.
During an inspection tour in China, Bethune cuts his finger on October 28 while performing surgery.	World War II is declared in September; Germany invades Poland; U.S.S.R. invades Poland and Finland and is expelled from League of Nations.
By November 5, Bethune's finger is infected; he dies of septicemia (blood poisoning) at 5:20 a.m. on November 12 at Huangshikou (Yellow Stone Pass).	In Canada, Joseph-Adélard Godbout succeeds Maurice Duplessis as Premier of Quebec.
1940	**1940**
Bethune's body moved to Chuch'eng to lie in state; 10,000 people pay respects.	Communist Party of Canada banned by War Measures Act and is re-formed as the Labour-Progressive Party.
	1941
	Germany invades U.S.S.R.; Japanese attack Pearl Harbour; U.S. and Britain declare war on Japan.
	In Canada, Dr. Frederick Banting dies.

BETHUNE AND HIS TIMES	CANADA AND THE WORLD

CANADA AND THE WORLD

1942
Murder of Jews in German-held concentration camps begins.

British researchers show that penicillin can be used to treat infections.

1945
U.S. President Roosevelt dies.

Spain excluded from the United Nations.

Fighting between Nationalists and Communists in northern China.

1946
Truce declared in Chinese Civil War.

1947
U.S. withdraws as mediator in China.

1949
Chiang Kai-shek resigns as President of China and removes forces to Formosa; The People's Republic of China proclaimed under Mao Tse-tung.

1950
Britain recognizes Communist China.

North Korea invades South Korea.

U.S. recognizes the new state of Vietnam.

BETHUNE AND HIS TIMES

CANADA AND THE WORLD

U.S. Congress places severe restrictions against members of the American Communist Party.

1952
In China, Bethune's body moved to park in Shijiazhuang; model hospital from Nin-Yen K'ou moved across the road from the park and renamed Norman Bethune International Peace Hospital.

1952
Effective anti-tuberculosis drugs come into use.

Acknowledgments
and
Recommended Further Reading

The words of Norman Bethune were taken, with permission, from two biographies: *The Scalpel, the Sword: the Story of Doctor Norman Bethune*, by Ted Allan and Sydney Gordon, (Toronto: McClelland & Stewart, 1952), and *Bethune*, by Roderick Stewart (Toronto: new press, 1973), and from a collection of photographs, letters, and writings by Bethune, covering his entire life: *The Mind of Norman Bethune*, by Roderick Stewart (Toronto: Fitzhenry & Whiteside, 1977). All three greatly influenced the picture I have attempted to paint of Bethune and his times, and I acknowledge my debt to them with gratitude.

Other publications to which I am grateful for background information and anecdotes about Bethune, are:

The Gallant Cause: Canadians in the Spanish Civil War 1936-1939 by Mark Zuelke. (Vancouver: Whitecap Books, 1996.) A compelling history of the hundreds of ordinary Canadians who risked everything to go and fight for a cause in which they believed.

Norman Bethune: his Times and his Legacy by David A.E. Shephard and Andrée Levesque (editors). (Ottawa: Canadian Public Health Association, 1982.) A collection of papers on Bethune and his times presented at a conference in 1979.

Bethune: The Montreal Years by Wendell MacLeod, Libbie Park and Stanley Ryerson. (Toronto: James Lorimer, 1978.) Diverse remembrances of Bethune from the early 1930s by three of his friends.
A Concise History of the Spanish Civil War by Gabriel Jackson. (London: Thames and Hudson, 1974.) An accessible, heavily illustrated, short, clear history of a complex and brutal war.
1915: The Death of Innocence by Lyn Macdonald. (London: Headline Book Publishing, 1993.) One in a fascinating series of oral histories of the First World War that Lyn Macdonald has put together from thousands of hours of reminiscences by the soldiers who actually took part.

Index

Almeria. *See* Malaga to Almeria road

Anarchism, 91, 93

Archibald, Dr. Edward (thoracic surgeon), 59, 61, 70

Artificial pneumothorax, 57-59, 61

Banting, Dr. Frederick (Bethune's classmate), 38, 79, 138, 149

Barcelona, Spain, 91, 95, 101

Bethune ancestors, 16-18, 19-21, 133, 134

Bethune, Elizabeth née Goodwin (Bethune's mother), 20, 24, 25, 26, 40, 134

Bethune, Frances Penney (Bethune's wife), 43-51, 57, 61, 106, 136, 140, 141, 142, 143, 144

Bethune, Henry Norman
appearance of, 23, 28
and the arts, 26, 28, 58, 61, 69, 71, 72-73, 146
attitude of colleagues toward, 61-62, 70, 71-72, 82
birth of, 17, 134
childhood of, 23-27, 135-36
and children, 62-63, 72-73, 101, 146, 147
in China, 14-15, 18-19, 111-23, 124, 128, 148
and communism, 79-81, 82-83, 105, 114, 128
courtship and marriages of, 41, 43-51, 141
death of, 14-15, 111, 124, 130, 148, 149, 151
designs surgical instruments, 60-61, 143

early employment of, 27-28, 136, 137
education and medical training of, 27, 28, 38, 39, 41, 46, 59-61, 136, 137, 138, 140, 141, 143
and health insurance, 81-82, 83, 128, 146
lifestyle of, 39-40
and Mao Tse-tung, 115
as a medical practitioner, 38, 40, 46-47, 58, 62-65, 71, 113-114, 120-21, 138, 139, 141, 142, 144, 147
in the military, 29, 31-39, 40-41, 138, 139
as a patient, 39, 55-58, 139
and his patients, 62-64, 120-21
personality of, 1-2, 3, 5, 10, 20-21, 23, 24, 25-26, 38, 39, 40, 47, 48-49, 56, 60, 61, 68-70, 77-78, 83, 100, 120
and religion, 25, 40
politics of, 73, 77-79, 81
posthumous fame of, 129-31
sense of humour of, 61, 67-68, 69-70
in Spain, 1-10, 86, 89-90, 94-101, 117, 128, 146
social life of, 67-68, 70, 72, 106, 123, 140
as a speaker, 78, 80, 82, 104-105, 123-24, 143, 144, 145, 147, 149
as a surgeon, 14-15, 26, 41, 60-62, 70, 82, 94, 116, 118, 119-21, 144, 149
and tuberculosis, 48, 55-58
See also Blood transfusions; Hospitals in China; "Pai-ch'iuen"

*Printed in December 2000
at Imprimerie Gauvin,
Hull (Québec).*